START AND GROW YOUR OWN CONSULTING BUSINESS FROM ZERO

A PROVEN 7-STEP GUIDE TO TURN YOUR EXPERTISE INTO INCOME, WIN CLIENTS FAST AND DEVELOP A MINDSET FOR SUCCESS

MATTHEW ROBSON

THE
CONSULTING
CLUB

CONTENTS

A SPECIAL BONUS TO OUR READERS

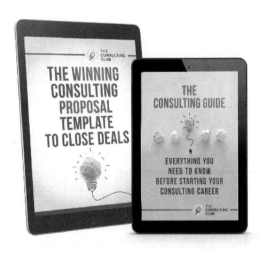

- **BONUS 1:** A Consulting Proposal Template to make sure to land all your deals.

- **BONUS 2:** A Consulting Guide For New Consultants with everything you need to know when starting your career.

Click here: https://theconsultingclub.com/free-resources

Alternatively, you can scan this QR code with your phone:

Also, make sure to join our Facebook Group Community to connect with other like-minded professionals:

https://www.facebook.com/groups/allaboutconsultingb

INTRODUCTION

There is an unspoken rule in the world of employment that a 9-to-5 job translates to stability, professional realization, and independence. A quick glance at the multitude of people stuck at a job they took fresh out of college or university just to make ends meet shows this simply isn't true. Not to mention the countless jobs lost during recessions and in the wake of the changing business landscape of the digital age.

So while having a full-time job is not without its benefits, the future is entrepreneurial. Starting your own business venture is certainly riskier, but it also comes with higher payoffs — the freedom to live and work anywhere in the world, a more rewarding career, more free time, and greater personal and professional fulfillment. This is where the limitless power of the Internet comes in! Never before has the entire world been just a click away. In business terms, this translates to pure gold. Just think about it – there are hundreds of thousands, even millions of potential customers out there. Just waiting for your guidance and professional opinion on how to navigate the entrepreneurial waters. All you need to do is learn how to reach them.

Many people don't realize it, but there is no better time than the one we live in to build a consulting business. The digital revolution opened the door to entrepreneurship to people who would otherwise spend their entire lives in the 9-to-5 format. And while some are happy with a steady job and knowing where their next paycheck comes from, others need something different. An entrepreneurial spirit comes with a certain level of restlessness and a penchant for risk. If you find yourself daydreaming at your current job, you may have the entrepreneur *'gene'*.

Now, before channeling those dreams and goals into actionable steps, let me tell you why hundreds of thousands of businesses are crying out for expertise from consultants:

- Save them time, make their business run more smoothly, and be more productive and efficient
- Market their products better and increase their sales
- Improve their social media, gain more visitors to their website, and ultimately increase their customer base
- Analyze their data to create reports and forecast future trends
- Assist the HR department, coach the leadership team, and so on

Many business challenges are connected to the ever-expanding and technologically complex digital world and to the market transformation, causing businesses to tear their hair out in frustration. Business owners are under a lot of pressure, often juggling multiple roles themselves with different hats to wear, and they can only do so much before this takes a toll on the business owner's health.[1] Often, businesses don't have the funds to employ someone to fill their knowledge gaps on how to make their business profitable and noticeable in the digital domain.[2] It's not always possible, and it's costly to have specific employees for every aspect of a business, and this is one of the reasons why they draw upon consultants.

Businesses usually focus on what they are really good at and lack time and knowledge to *'think outside'* of the box, keep up with trends and disruptive consumer demand. Over the years, I have seen many new business owners fail because of wishful thinking. They have the idea, the passion, and the drive but fall short in the execution. They lack the *'blueprint'* to make their business profitable and noticeable in the digital domain. And doing that starts with research and ends with hard work and perseverance.

Too many entrepreneurs skip the first part and doom their business from the start by picking an over-saturated or not profitable niche. It seems like a simple mistake to avoid, but it's also a common pitfall. I also saw lots of businesses not succeeding over time simply because they missed to plan the *'future'*. From small to large companies, hiring a consultant can be a huge time-saver and a real asset to growth while removing direct pressure from business owners.[3] I personally view a business consultant as a medical doctor for every company, regardless of the field; they observe, diagnose a problem, then provide a remedy to ease the issue and consult the client on how to *'stay healthy'* and embrace a lifestyle.

WHY I AM WRITING THIS BOOK

I am writing this book because I have also been there and managed to build my own successful consulting business from scratch. It's been a lot of hard work, but it has been incredibly rewarding. I feel a huge sense of achievement to know that I've created this myself and have helped so many businesses along the way. I remember when I was starting out, despite ten years of experience in corporate and consulting work for start-ups, I wasn't exactly sure where to start. I remember that terror, fear, self-doubt, and a feeling of being out of my depth at times. Initially, I was even uncertain about which niche I should go into. I was worried about how I would finance the business and make enough income to live on while the company found its feet. **Do these feelings sound familiar?**

I didn't do everything right the first time. I made mistakes and had failures. But I was always happy and interested to learn, develop, grow, and improve. Now I want to give something back, as all my mentors, coaches, experts, consultants, colleagues, and friends helped me along the way. I want to make things easier and quicker for **you** so that you can build your business while avoiding the mistakes I made.

Building my own business is the best thing I've ever done! I have broken away from the 9-5 culture, and I can proudly say I have reached the so-called *'financial freedom'*. I now have more time and the financial resources to spend time on things that make me feel alive.

THE BEST TIME TO START IS NOW

In 2021, the consulting industry generated $200.6 billion and grew by 5.2% yearly over the past five years.[4] It's a growing area with significant demand; there is definitely room for you to have a piece of that market by starting and growing your own consulting business. In case you need more reassurance, let's take a look at some more factors contributing to this rising demand:

Impact of Covid — Because of the COVID-19 pandemic, it is expected that economic recovery will drive industry revenue, and there will be an increase in budgets that allows companies to spend even more on consulting services. In 2021, US consultants saw an uptick in demand from technology businesses because companies needed tailored solutions to facilitate people working from home.

Globalization — The world, in general, is changing. With many companies providing projects overseas, they have the challenge to deliver projects faster, more efficiently, with tighter budgets, yet still retaining customer satisfaction. All the changes in the world do open up more opportunities for consulting firms, as businesses want help and guidance from experts to map out future strategies.

Technological changes — Companies need to restructure operations to become more digital and resilient to future disruptions.

US volatile markets and regulation changes — Because of the highly volatile market and its constant government regulation reforms, management consultants are often required to help businesses navigate this changing landscape.[5]

MISCONCEPTIONS ABOUT CONSULTING

As I have shown you, there are many good reasons businesses should hire a small consulting firm. Still, there is also an untapped market of companies that aren't yet hiring consultants because they hold misconceptions. It's worth being aware of these from the outset so that you can work on challenging them and educating business owners on how you could help their businesses. It is also essential to take these into account while developing your business model and value proposition:

Failing businesses — Some people believe that you only need the help of a consultant if the business is failing. But companies that are already doing well also benefit hugely from consultants to improve their business further and take it to the next level.

Consulting is only for large businesses — Some people think that consulting is only required for large and established businesses. This misconception forgets that when a company is just starting out, it can really benefit from mentorship to steer it in the right direction and ensure that it becomes sustainable. Consulting can also help a business to keep up with the pace of the market.

Consultants are costly — Some people think that consultants are really expensive. There are different types of consulting, from large ongoing jobs to small one-off projects. Consultants with their expertise can give a great return on investment *(ROI)*, meaning that whatever client's spend on consulting fees is well worth the value they bring back into the business over time.

Consultants advise then depart — Some clients fear that a consultant will give generic advice that may not fit their business, but a good consultant will help implement and embed the solutions for clients. Consultancy nowadays can often be about developing multi-year relationships so that you have better insight into the business and can steer it to transformation. It's about a long-term client relationship.[6]

Consultants aren't experts in the sector — Some businesses may wonder why you could help them if you aren't an industry expert. As a consultant, you are an expert in your area but can apply those transferable skills, new knowledge, concepts, and innovations in similar industries and companies.[7]

BUSINESSES NEED YOU!!!

Small businesses may initially want or have to do everything themselves and be a jack of all trades, but this doesn't mean they do everything well. They can't be experts at everything, and while, in some cases, they've maybe done enough just to muddle by, there will come a time where just getting by isn't good enough, and they'll either make no more progress with their business or start to fall behind in some areas. This is why companies need you.

Businesses may want to grow and take the next step forward but are unsure about how to do this. Business consultants often spend some time observing how the company currently runs and then create innovative and time-saving solutions that will make the business run smoother or bring more sales.[8] In other words, you can act as a catalyst for change.

HOW THIS BOOK WILL HELP YOU

"Be your own boss and start early."

— BILL GATES, MICROSOFT

In this book, I will guide you through the journey of becoming a business consultant from zero. I will give you the skills to break out of the corporate world and enter the world of small business by utilizing the knowledge and expertise you have previously acquired. Make your consulting firm your primary source of income and be successful by making a career out of it. By the end of reading this book, you will have a solid business plan in place.

So, without further ado, let's get started on this exciting journey and move into Chapter 1, learning how to think like an entrepreneur.

1

THINKING LIKE AN
ENTREPRENEUR

"An entrepreneur is someone who jumps off a cliff and builds a plane on the way down."

— REID HOFFMAN, LINKEDIN

T hinking like an entrepreneur is the very first step when starting this new journey of building your own consulting business.

You might ask yourself why you need to work on your mindset, but believe me, this has been the cornerstone of not only my success but every business owner I know. Entrepreneurs think differently from many because they produce innovative ideas and solutions and have the bravery to start and grow their own business from zero by working hard and making sacrifices to achieve massive success. This first chapter will help you think like an entrepreneur by teaching you how to embrace a growth mindset, allow yourself to fail, and develop your new company. When you have a business-oriented mindset, you will create opportunities for entrepreneurship and act, even when things are uncertain. You will learn through the actions you take, reflecting, experimenting, and always moving forward to your goal.[1] This chapter will get you started on becoming a self-made entrepreneur by outlining *eight mindset shifts* that successful business people must make to achieve their ultimate goal.

By the end of the chapter, you will:

1. See the benefits of changing your habits for a lifetime.
2. Understand the benefits of making sacrifices in the short term to achieve your end-game.
3. Learn how living in the present and planning for the future is far more productive than dwelling on past mistakes or situations.
4. Understand that regardless of your past, this does not define your future.
5. Be enthused and committed to growing and improving to achieve your dreams.
6. Be able to define your why. Why do you want to start your own business?
7. Be OK if you fail at certain aspects of your journey to your goals.
8. Learn some of the Dos and Don'ts from lots of tips from experts.

CHANGE HABITS

I once came across a book that profoundly impacted the way I think about sacrifices; it's called Principles: Life and Work, where *Ray Dalio* says:

"Imagine that to have a great life, you have to cross a dangerous jungle. You can stay safe and have an ordinary life or risk

2

crossing the jungle to have a remarkable life. How would you approach that choice? Take a moment to think about it because it is the sort of choice that, in one form or another, we all have to make."[2]

The day I read this quote, I wrote my resignation letter. I did not send it until years later, but I knew that day would come. I knew I had to make sacrifices to stop having the kind of life all my childhood friends were leading. There is nothing wrong with that kind of comfortable life; don't take me wrong. I just realized it was not for me.

For me, an entrepreneur's success is primarily due to their core values and character, but also, their habits. A great piece of advice I would never forget says:

"Be careful of your deeds, for your deeds become your habits; Be careful of your habits, for your habits become your character; Be careful of your character, for your character becomes your destiny."[3]

Indeed, I have tested in my own flesh that what you do becomes habitual and will eventually transform into what you become in the future. It can be tough to break a habit and start a new routine. If you keep practicing a new habit over and over, it will eventually become part of your lifestyle and be instinctive for you. But careful, you will need attention, determination, and willpower to develop good entrepreneurial patterns.

Good and Bad habits

Realizing and understanding that you have bad habits is the first important step to changing them.

Take some time to think now about the BAD habits you'd like to change that prevent you from being the entrepreneur you want and the GOOD habits you'd like to develop that would make you more successful and will bring you closer to your goal.

Brandon Bornancin, an inspiring author, entrepreneur, and *'sales monster'*, has a valuable chapter in his book on habits. When you're analyzing your life and trying to ensure that the patterns in your life are good, he suggests asking four questions about whether the activity you're doing will:

1. Improve your wealth?
2. Improve your health?
3. Improve your opportunity to be the best you can be and achieve your aims?
4. Have a positive effect on one billion people?[4]

Developing **good habits**, and getting rid of **bad habits**, is looking at your life, behavior, and actions to ensure that you're always getting closer to what you want to accomplish.

BAD habits could include things like giving up too soon if things don't go smoothly immediately, not giving yourself time to think, reflect, be creative and develop, letting your time get taken up with other demands *(work colleagues, family)*; procrastinating *(watching TV, playing computer games, drinking at a pub)*; not delegating or drawing upon expertise but instead making the mistake that you have to do everything; not investing in your future today.

GOOD habits could include things like: exercise or meditation to keep your body and mind healthy and firing on all cylinders, setting aside business development/strategy/vision time, having time to reflect, or getting up half an hour or an hour earlier in the morning. I personally love waking up at 5 am because I feel like I am working towards my dreams while most of the world is still sleeping. Other good habits I try to implement in my daily routine include making a *'to-do'* list for the next day in the evening so that I start the next day with a clear focus. I would also try to attend networking events and turn off the notifications on my phone during working hours so I don't lose focus.

I learned that we can break down good and bad habits into four components:

1. **A Prompt/Trigger**
2. **A Craving**
3. **Your Action**
4. **The Reward**

Take time to choose a bad habit and consider these four components. For example, a bad habit could be spending too much time checking emails, which constantly distracts your focus. The prompt would be the ping of the email arriving in your inbox. The craving is the desire to check the email. Your action is you decide to check it instead of leaving it until the allocated email time. The reward is the relief of having checked it.

Then, do the same with a good habit.

An example of a good habit could be waking up early to work out before your working day starts. The prompt could be the thought of the endorphins going through your body. A craving is the feeling that you will get to accomplish something before your workday even starts. Your action is you decide to set up the alarm and commit to it. The reward is that you'll feel better, more productive, and with a great sense of accomplishment.

A way to change a bad habit can include changing the trigger for the bad habit; for example, in the scenario where a person interrupts their day by constantly checking emails or social media, the trigger is the *'pinging'* sounds of emails or social media. Changing the *'trigger'* could be switching off the notification sound. You could try to view the habit as unpleasant. You can try to make it harder to act if, for example, you were trying to break the habit of checking up on your phone constantly. You could put the phone in another room and set an alarm every X hours to check it. I realized that I was constantly distracted by the presence of my phone so I decided to give this a try. You cannot imagine how my brain was sending me constant signals to check out my phone, even when it was no longer in the same room!

Ways to start a new habit include prompting yourself with an automatic reminder or a visual motivation. Make the prompt attractive. Make it easy to make the habit. If you need tools to help you get these, or if you need the encouragement of a friend or colleague, ask for their help too. Ensure that you reward yourself for making your good habit. If the routine doesn't have its benefits, ensure you recompense yourself by doing something you enjoy.

BE WILLING TO MAKE SACRIFICES

You will inevitably have to make sacrifices If you're thinking of becoming an entrepreneur. This could be that you don't spend as much time with family and friends or on hobbies, and this is tough because you will most likely feel guilt, even though you know you're doing it for a better future. With sacrifice, you frequently give up short-term pleasure for long-term satisfaction.

For example, when I started building my own business, I saw my friends having fun on the weekends, going to parties, and enjoying the sun outside. I was stuck inside, working on my computer, and if I joined dinner, I would stick to water and leave early to make sure I was performing the day after. I won't lie, it was a short-term sacrifice of *'fun'*, but the long-term result is that I could build my dream career. There is good advice for doing something today to help your future self, which can be through many different decisions you make with habits or wiser choices.

A great example of entrepreneurial sacrifice is Jeff Bezos, who quit his stable and lucrative Wall Street job to found Amazon. He sacrificed financial and emotional security and stability for calculated risk, which really paid off. He didn't want to miss out on the *"path not taken."*[5]

"If you always do what you've always done, you will always get what you've always got."

This phrase has been attributed to various people, including Henry Ford, Jessie Potter, and Tony Robbins. Maybe you are stuck in your 9 am – 5 pm job and are fed up with your life, but if you are honest to yourself, you are probably not making any changes in your habits or taking any risks that involve any kind of sacrifice.

≈ ≈ ≈

Action Points:

- Have a go at defining the bad habits you'd like to change and good habits you'd like to develop:

1. Bad Habits to change/eliminate
Example: Start turning off your mobile phone to avoid distracting pings from social media

---

2. Good Habits to develop
Example: Make a list of priority tasks to be done the next day, at the

end of your working day ... so you're organized, know your plan, and ready to go the next morning.

3. What sacrifices are you willing to make?

Example: I am willing to sacrifice 1 hour in bed; and get up at 5:30am instead of 6:30am, to make use of the quiet time to have space to make strategic plans for the business.

YOUR PAST DOES NOT DEFINE YOUR FUTURE

We all come from diverse backgrounds and may have had to overcome different challenges in our life. If you had a challenging childhood or were born into a low social-economic area, this does not define your future. I was lucky enough to have a comfortable childhood and have my career and master's degree paid for by my parents. I understand that this is not the case for everyone.

However, there are plenty of examples out there: **Sundar Pichai**, the CEO of Google, came from a family in India that was not wealthy. The children did not have their bedrooms but slept in the living room of a 2-room apartment. Pichai had a natural talent for recalling numbers from memory. He learned how to write computer programs and won a scholarship to Stanford. He later gained a job with Google and worked on their search toolbar; then Chrome, and over time was asked to head up different departments. If you want to start and grow your own consulting business and be a massive success, you CAN! You just need to do it. Nothing is stopping you! It is sensible, however, to develop a flexible mindset to deal with uncertainty, change and to be prepared to roll with those changes and gain opportunities from them.

To get into an entrepreneurial mindset, you need to acknowledge that how things have worked in the past is not necessarily how they'll work in the future. Therefore you will need to constantly reinvent yourself and your business.

We, entrepreneurs, are in charge of creating the future, offering innovative products and services. However, no one teaches you how to deal with uncertainty. No one tells you that you'll have to work harder than anyone else, try new things, fail, learn and start again. All of this with constant uncertainty. Is all the sacrifice worth it? Is my product going to work? Yes, it's true, an entrepreneur's future is uncertain; you won't have a big corporation writing you the checks by the end of the month. But hey, that's the beauty of it. **You won't have extraordinary results by doing what everyone else does, right?**

You need to develop a mindset that will help you achieve success. First of all, ensure that your consumer is central to your business and create a benefit for them. Consumers are central to everything, start from them and work backward while anticipating their needs. As an entrepreneur today, you need to develop a mission and value proposition that focuses on and positively impacts people's lives *(I'll cover more of this in the next chapter)*. What value can you provide to consumers? Think about this long-term and try not to get embroiled in the short-term issues.

. . .

When you're defining your future and thinking about your destiny, I suggest you dream big and prepare for significant achievements. By doing so, your actions will start to match your thoughts, and without even noticing, you'll set yourself up for success. **Dare to dream big, and you will achieve it.**

🚀 🚀 🚀

Action Point:

- Write what your BIG dream is:

Example: My dream is to start & grow a consulting business for the Visitor Economy sector, advising customers on how to improve footfall to the attractions, membership pricing structures, design of hospitality venues, day, and seasonal events etc.

COMMIT TO CONSTANT GROWTH AND IMPROVEMENT

Commit to constant growth and improvement and make it your life motto. Look at what changes you can make to improve and force yourself to constantly think about where you are going and what may be required in the future.

A great case study of this concept is Mate Rimac, who, at the age of 19, replaced a faulty engine with an electric one. He had the vision to know that in the future environmental concerns and regulations would see a place for electric vehicles, so he founded a company to produce electric cars. His company is very successful and employs over 350 people.[6]

Once you have a goal and a vision, you should over-commit to it. Brandon Bornancin explains it very well in his book; if you have a purpose, you should eliminate everything that takes your focus away from achieving that goal.[7] This could be switching off distracting TVs or music channels. It could be cutting down on social commitments until a project is finished etc.

🚀 🚀 🚀

Action Points:

- Fill the boxes below:

1. **What barriers/distractions are getting in your way of focusing on your goal?**
Example: If lack of time was a barrier, try to free up time by delegating tasks to others.

```



```

2. **What improvements do you want your business to make?**
Example: The company websites could be made more accessible to a wider audience, with text to speech, and translation into other languages.

DEFINE YOUR WHY. WHY DO YOU WANT TO START YOUR OWN BUSINESS?

"He who has a why, can endure any how."

— FREDERICK NIETZSCHE

There will be a reason behind your wanting to start your consulting business. The reason does not really matter here, but you need to be connected to that reason so that it gives you a purpose, a cause, and a belief that drives you to act and fulfill your goal. This is what is called **your motive to act.**[8] Sometimes you may need to reflect on it and remind yourself why you're doing it because, I am telling you, it will be hard work. It will take every ounce of your strength, resilience, and determination.[9] Knowing *'your WHY'* will help you to commit to your dream.[10]

Steve Jobs claimed that each morning he looked in the mirror and asked himself if this was the last day he lived, would he want to do what he intended to spend the day doing. If his answer was *'no'* too often, he knew he had to make some changes.[11]

In case you need them, I've put together some reasons why you 'may' want to start your own consulting business:

- You like working for yourself; you want to be your own boss and set your hours and priorities.
- You may feel you have a wealth of experience you'd like to share because you want to help others succeed and thrive.
- You want the satisfaction of building a successful business.
- You want to earn money and financial independence.
- You want to use your creativity.
- You want to change your life to improve things for yourself and your family.
- You want a business that you can sell in the future to make a significant profit.
- You want freedom – freedom of choice, freedom of decisions, freedom to work differently or live a lifestyle you choose.
- For most people, it is more than money that drives them, and sometimes asking the question: *"If money was not a factor at all, what would you decide to do with your life?"* helps them to identify their WHY. Another question I asked myself in the past was, *"what do you love to do that makes you feel excited?"* Whatever that is, try to do more of that and build a career/business you love around it.

If you're struggling to know what area to focus on for a business, ask friends and family what you're good at. Consider what people ask you to help them with frequency, which could be an area where you decide to set up a consulting business.

Once you have a reason WHY... this will allow you to focus on your long-term plans and not let anything get in the way. You may make few profits initially, but you will keep at it because of this long-term plan.[12]

🐾 🐾 🐾

Action Point:

Knowing why will constantly guide you as you reach toward making your dreams a reality. Knowing your reason will help give you clarity, meaning, and fulfillment so that you start living in alignment with your purpose.

- Take some time to think about your reasons why now, and write them in the box below

Example: I have a product/service that I believe in, and I believe is the best out there. I have experience. Great customer reviews. I believe I can genuinely add value to customers. I want to work for myself and take work that I enjoy so work is a pleasure and not onerous. It's more rewarding knowing that every penny you earn, is because you've created the business opportunity.

EMBRACE FAILURE: HOW FALLING SHORT SETS YOU UP FOR SUCCESS

"I have not failed. I've just found 10,000 ways that won't work."
– Thomas Edison

"Success is a lousy teacher. It seduces smart people into thinking they can't lose."
– Bill Gates, Microsoft

"We do lots of Stuff. The only way you are going to have success is to have lots of failures first."

– Sergey Brin, Google[13]

When something in your business fails, and a mistake is made, this isn't a reason for sadness. Instead, you can learn from it and use it as a competitive advantage that your business has over others.[14] When mistakes are made, you as a leader become a stronger person, and your team will be more successful in the future because you can learn from what went wrong so it isn't repeated.

When I was starting my business, a ton of things went wrong along the way. And this will happen to you, or at least, I wish it will. I have never learned more or pushed myself further out of my comfort zone than after a big failure. Every failure has lessons to be learned, and they transform into opportunities if you approach them creatively. When I started my business, I could not get any big clients in my first six months. I lived this as a big failure. I was focusing my pitch on selling myself as a consultant instead of spending that valuable time with the customer to understand its needs and how I could help them. This failure forced me to stop, re-evaluate and reinvent myself. What would have happened if I got a couple of clients during these six months? I would have never tried to bring a better version to the table. Failure will occur; I recommend embracing it and using it to forge your best self.

One of the numerous times I failed, I read a study from Himadri Barman, and I saw this quote:

"Failure is a reality check to move forward, not an excuse to fall behind!"

He suggests that people should learn from failure and carry on towards their goals. He recommends a **3 R approach** to overcome fail-

15

ure: **Rewind** — *look back and understand what went wrong,* **Rediscover** *– can it work differently?* And finally, **Rework** *– get back to work with enthusiasm and determination to beat failure.*[15]

If you don't fail, you may not be taking enough risks. Sometimes you can be proactive and take a risk; if it works, it will ultimately give you a competitive advantage. Try things out, and challenge yourself, test ideas, make discoveries.[16] Sometimes you may find that the assumptions you held before testing them were wrong.

If there is a failure in your company, change the mindset from brushing it under the carpet and ignoring it, and instead talk about it, celebrate it, and learn from it. Ensure that your company culture accepts that things will fail and treats it like a learning experience. If you fail as a leader, share it with the team, so they feel happy to share too. Have a non-blame culture. Try to understand that sometimes, time and money will be lost. Be optimistic about the failure and say: *"we've learned a valuable lesson today that we wouldn't have known about!"* If something hasn't worked, it's something to build upon, improve, and get better at. When you fail, you develop skills of resilience and problem-solving!

Chinese entrepreneur **Jack Ma** failed exams at school. He gained only one point out of 120 on the math section of his college entrance exam. He was rejected from Harvard ten times but maintained patience and persistence. Over 30 jobs rejected him, and when 24 people applied to work for KFC, 23 people were hired, but not Jack Ma. He struggled to get funding for Alibaba, and it didn't make a profit for the first three years. Early on, he made a significant error in telling his partners they could not expect to rise to a higher position than a manager. His lesson from this was to value his team, let it be innovative, and have a vision.[17] Jack Ma was ultimately very successful. His failures shaped him into who he is and gave him great strength, resilience, and determination. Failures aren't significant setbacks; they're just a tiny piece of the larger end-game. All failures also contain the seeds of success.[18]

$$\wp \quad \wp \quad \wp$$

Action Point:

- Think of any area in life where you have *'failed'* previously. Reflect upon this and think of some positives.

1. A previous failure

Example: I ran an online Action Learning Challenge workshop, and two delegates dropped out.

2. Lessons learned?

Example: Not to take things too personally. That learning style doesn't suit everyone; and sometimes people have other life-events going on that need to take priority. Perhaps make a video for the future to show prospective attendees what the workshops are like, and stress the commitment required.

"If something is important enough, or you believe something is important enough, even if you are scared, you will keep going."
— **Elon Musk, Tesla Motors**

"I don't think you can invent on behalf of customers unless you're willing to think long-term because much invention doesn't work. If you're going to invent, it means you're going to experiment, and if you're going to experiment, you're going to fail, and if you're going to fail, you have to think long term."
– **Jeff Bezos, Amazon**

"Ideas aren't fully formed and only become clear as you work on them. You just have to get started."
– **Mark Zuckerberg, Meta**

"Passion, creativity, and resilience are the most crucial business skills. If you've got those, you're ready to embark on the journey."
— **Jo Malone, Jo Malone**

"You have to see failure as the beginning and the middle, but never entertain it as an end."
– **Jessica Herrin, Stella & Dot**

"I can name dozens of failures that we had over the years. Yet, with all these failures, we still managed to build Appster into one of our industry's largest and best companies. So, remember every time you fail, remind yourself these words: *Life won't always go my way, but I will always find a way.*"
— **Josiah Humphrey, Appster**

The next chapter will assess your area of expertise and help you determine your niche. The chapter will help you identify your target audience and their pain points *(the issue/problem)*, which your product or service can solve for them. The chapter will help you develop a smart goal and a value proposition for your business that will show the positive impact you intend on your target group.

KEY TAKEAWAYS FROM THIS CHAPTER

1. Discuss the good habits you'd like to have and the bad ones you would like to eliminate – work on increasing/decreasing these, respectively.
2. Dream big and strive towards this.
3. Remember that your past does not define your future, and always be flexible with whatever comes your way in life, deal with uncertainty and changes by viewing them as opportunities.
4. Give thought to why you want to start a business; this will drive you to action and keep you motivated.
5. Be prepared to fail, learn, and look for the opportunities in failure.

THE BASICS: ASSESS YOUR EXPERTISE AND DETERMINE YOUR NICHE

The second step in starting and growing your consulting business is assessing your expertise and determining your niche. *"See a need, fill a need"* needs to be your mentality. Through this chapter, I'll show you how to identify your target audience and assess their pain points.

What is the problem that they are currently facing? What keeps them awake at night? How does this make them feel? This second chapter will teach you how to write your business's SMART goals, value propositions, and mission statements and address the questions above accordingly.

By the end of this chapter, you will be able to:

1. State clearly and concisely your area of expertise.
2. Know which audience your products or services are intended for.
3. Understand what your customer's pain points are.
4. Conduct productive market research to better understand the industry and competition.

5. Define your competitive advantage, your Unique Selling Point *(USP)*.
6. Critically and objectively assess whether the business is a viable opportunity.
7. Create SMART goals.
8. Make a value proposition outlining what promise of value or benefits you can offer your customers.
9. Devise a meaningful mission statement that will guide you, your staff, and business throughout every step, from start-up, right into the future.

DETERMINE WHAT YOU DO

In this first part of the chapter, I will guide you to determine your area of expertise. I believe passion plays a crucial role in defining your area of competence because if you are not genuinely passionate about running a business in a specific area, you should probably take another path. Below are some questions you can ask yourself that may help you determine what you love and are good at:

1. What are your qualifications?
2. What is your experience?
3. What are your skills or expertise that could add value?
4. What skills or experience help you to stand out from the crowd?
5. How could your skills and experience benefit others?
6. What do people regularly ask you to help them with?[1]
7. What do you enjoy doing?
8. What tasks at work are you eager to take on?
9. What roles do you like to do, even if you don't get paid?
10. What empowers you?
11. What are you good at naturally?
12. What were you good at as a child?
13. Do people give you compliments that you don't take seriously enough?

14. Do you have skills that have helped you to excel in life or that have helped you to defeat any barriers in your way?[2]

McKinsey is an excellent example of how a company was created after its founder's expertise. The company was founded in 1925 when James O. McKinsey used his accounting expertise to help businesses. He was a professor at the University, and because of his accounting and management skills, he got many consulting jobs on the side. As he got more project proposals, he hired consultants to work for him, eventually becoming a key player in the accounting field.[3]

Once you have identified your skills, try to offer your services for free to 2-3 companies so that you have this experience to use as an example when you start charging for your consulting services. You can give definite statements such as: *"I have helped three companies to improve X and Y."*

DETERMINE WHO YOU DO IT FOR

You will need to consider to whom you will offer your consulting services and how. For example, you need to choose whether you are offering a one-off session or a long-term strategy *(if long-term, a retainer arrangement may work better)*.

For things like advertising and social media, you need to know for whom you're creating content so that your message is as impactful as possible. You need to understand what social media channels to use, what to post about, what topics, and what words or language will appeal to your audience.[4]

When considering whom you're doing it for, it is worth considering who could benefit from your knowledge or expertise. You need to consider their personality, age, what they do for fun, where they shop, whether they spend their time online or offline, if they use social media, what time they have available, what products they use, *etc.* Perhaps consider brain-storming ideas, as you may find different audiences you hadn't initially contemplated. **It is essential to keep testing and refining what you do and create a solid picture of your ideal customer in your mind.**

Doing this will better understand how your product or services would fit in with their life.[5] It would help to consider your current clients, those you want to reach, and your dream clients. It's beneficial to use their words to describe their problems, not your own because this will help you to understand their thinking patterns and help you reach them when you do marketing. If there are things you don't know yet about your customers, **be prepared to do market research** to find them out.[6]

❧ ❧ ❧

Action Points:

- Fill the boxes below with your thoughts:

1. What are you an Expert at? What will you Consult on?
Example: Perhaps you have 12 years of experience in cybersecurity?

```



```

2. Who is your Audience?
Example: Any companies that use ICT, and who want to protect the information they hold.

```



```

DETERMINE THE PAIN POINTS THAT YOUR TARGET AUDIENCE HAS AND WHAT THEY WANT TO ACHIEVE

A *'pain point'* means a problem that customers experience.[7] Their pain point could fall into four key categories:

1. A problem that is currently costing them too much money.
2. A problem that is taking up too much of their time.
3. A problem with a complicated process that needs to be refined.
4. A problem that lacks support.

Looking at the four scenarios directly above, you could ask yourself questions that relate to the four points:

1. If the customer's pain point is cost — can you offer a lower price or the savings they'll make, or show why they will get a good return on investment *(ROI)*?

2. If the customer's pain point is lack of time – can you show how you could save their time and make the process easier?

3. If the customer's pain point is a complicated procedure needing refinement — can you make completing the task easier or integrate something with a current produce/service to make it run more smoothly? Or speed up time-intensive tasks?

4. If the customer's pain point is lack of support — can you make them feel supported and like a partner with language such as *'us'* and *'we'*?

Osterwalder describes customer pains as things that annoy them before, throughout, or after doing a job or something that prevents them from doing it.[8] Knowing a customer's pain points allows you to position your company in a way that will provide the solution to their problems.

. . .

Airbnb is a well-known example of a company that took advantage of the customer pain point of not having enough hotel rooms in San Francisco and came up with the idea of Airbnb by working backward from the customer's need to a solution. They bought some airbeds and offered people breakfast for a charge of $80 a night. The idea worked! (It wasn't all smooth sailing, and they had to be inventive and sell cereals to fund their start-up; the pictures of places weren't great, so they bought a camera to take better photos). Their perseverance and constant striving to make improvements paid off.[9]

Customer pain points are as diverse as people, and these are an excellent indicator of what drives urgency for their businesses. A deep understanding of your customer pain points will help your consulting business deliver better solutions than competitors. Here are some suggestions for how you could try to pinpoint these:

It is worth doing qualitative research

Where you allow customers to respond to open questions, rather than just quantitative *(which is easier to draw statistics from but gives you less value in understanding your customer).*

You need to listen carefully to your customers

You need to ensure that customers are focused on the issues/problems that you have the potential to solve. You could hold focus groups with customers and ask them to share their honest experiences, positive and negative, so that you can learn from this and better meet their needs.

You can do quantitative research

Via surveys if you want to get evidence to support that you are in touch with your customer's pain points. For example, if you suspect your customer's most significant pain point is time management, survey results support this; you can use relevant statistics in your marketing and choose words focused on *'saving time.'* If you can show customers that when they have their pain point solved by you, this will also help them in other ways, *i.e.,* to be more productive or to gain more customers/sales, this will also help.

An essential tip is not just to lower your prices to compete with their current service provider. Instead, you could offer a monthly subscription plan at a lower price or emphasize the added value you will provide and how satisfied your customers are, which shows they'll get a good return on investment *(ROI).*

Showing customer testimonials/reviews on your website/literature is an excellent way to demonstrate that you have resolved other customers' pain points. It's always worth gathering these.[10] I highly recommend asking your current customers for these if you don't have any. For anyone whom you know that you've done a fantastic job, going above and beyond with the service you've provided, prompt them to ask if they could take the time to leave a review or a *'quote'* that you can use. Often, it is beneficial to them too, as it advertises their business at the same time.

🐾 🐾 🐾

Action Points:

- Take a chance to complete the boxes below:

1. What are your customer's pain points?
Example: They teach in-person workshops, but would like to expand to online learning, but don't have the skills/expertise.

[blank box]

2. What is your solution? How will their business improve in other ways?

Example: I have years of experience of creating e-learning and running workshops. I have the technical know-how. I would support them to create online learning. By having online learning too, this will bring in an additional revenue stream into their company which enables them to expand and develop.

[blank box]

3. Do you have any reviews/testimonials?

Example: Yes lots, see my website from named individuals, who have given their permission for me to use their name and company.

[blank box]

MARKET RESEARCH (UNDERSTAND THE INDUSTRY AND THE COMPETITION)

Now that you know your customer pain points let's move into market research to understand the industry and your competition. *Osterwalder* talks about being observant of customers to ensure that the characteristics you assume they have can be observed and verified. It's like testing a scientific hypothesis; you have an idea and then need to prove it's a correct assumption.[11] So, it's well worth doing thorough market research to understand the industry, your potential customers, and your competition.

Tom Searcy advises that rather than showing that you're *better* than competitors, ensure that you target customers that will be the perfect fit for your product/services.[12]

Jeff Bezos, CEO of Amazon, has a similar mentality. He believes that if you are obsessed with your competitors, you've already lost out because if you are the leader and you are competitor-focused, where will you get your energy from? You lose sight of what is essential. He suggests instead that it's best to focus on your team and customers. He doesn't mean ignoring competitors, but using them to make you more motivated, not anxious. He suggests staying focused on the customer and letting competitors focus on you.[13]

Jeff Bezos' idea of focusing on the customer is one of the famous core values of Amazon, *"work backward from the customer, rather than starting with an idea for a product and trying to bolt customers onto it."* If customers are not excited about or view what you're offering as beneficial, then perhaps continue your research.

Be customer-driven rather than competitor driven

Ensure you know who your perfect customer would be. Know the problem that you can resolve for the customer. Be the expert for this customer. 2021 research by *Henriikka Forstadius* shows the importance of conducting a market review and looking at the broader market context, including some historical context and deep diving into niches, looking at customer profiling, market positioning, and ensuring a customer-centric business model.[14] It is essential to conduct this research to ensure your business idea is brilliant and emotionally intelligent. It is easy to like an opinion because you have spent time, effort, and money on it. Still, by working back from the customer and testing the idea out with them, you can refine the idea and get it right so that it works for customers and is thriving.

When I am conducting a market research, I like to think of a single customer and create a solution for that single person. This helps me to focus on details and don't get lost in all the information. If I manage to help one customer, there are probably thousands of others out there with the same issue and necessities.

🖉 🖉 🖉

Action Points:

- Take a moment to complete the boxes below:

1. Who are your competitors?
Example: A, B, C Online Tutors

>

2. What do you offer that they don't?

Example: Tutors with global connections in China, US, and Europe – so a much wider reaching model

KEYS TO BECOMING AN EXPERT (DEFINE YOUR COMPETITIVE ADVANTAGE)

One of the key ways to become an expert is to ensure that you have a competitive advantage. A competitive advantage is something that your company has that allows you to provide a service, product, or skill better than your competitors.[15] **Your competitors shouldn't be able to fulfill your role quickly; if they can, you don't have a competitive advantage.**

Some examples of competitive advantage could include you having resources that other competitors don't have. You may have a highly skilled workforce; you could be in a unique location; you could have new technology that you own; you may be able to produce products at the lowest cost, or you could have a brand that is very well recognized. People are often relatively passive about knowing their competency niches, perhaps out of modesty, cultural upbringing, or maybe not learning to identify competencies. Still, understanding areas of strength can mean that any changes can be dealt with swiftly and opportunities grasped because people's competitive advantages are known.[16]

Some practical examples of competitive advantage could be that you ideally need to offer something at a lower cost than your competitors *(an example of this would be McDonald's)* or have a product or service that is different from your competitors. This could be either high-quality or innovative *(an example of this is Louis Vuitton)*, or you need to be focused on a specific area so that you have a niche *(an example of this could be a specialist cacti shop)*. Some things that have worked for me in the past to develop a competitive advantage include:

1. Ensuring you or your staff have skills that others don't *(this is a strong argument here for investing in your staff training and development to keep skills updated and cutting-edge)*.
2. Having an innovative product or service.
3. Developing your brand.
4. Take time to understand your and your staff's competency niches.

❧ ❧ ❧

Action Point:

- Make a note of what your competitive advantage is. What do you do better/differently compared to other companies?

Example: Our company offers sector specialist Business Advisors, for the Visitor Economy, or Manufacturing sectors with years of experience – high quality practical experience.

DETERMINE AND ASSESS WHAT MAKES THIS AN OPPORTUNITY

It's essential to evaluate whether you have identified a good business opportunity. Some key factors to help you assess this include:

1. Looking at the market size, which you will have done as part of your market research. How likely are people to pay for the service or product you offer?
2. Consider cash flow practically, and ensure the business can be sustainable after some time.
3. Consider your skillsets and those of your colleagues/partners/employees *(if you will employ people)*. Are there any skill areas currently lacking that you will need to acquire?
4. Does everyone connected to your business have the commitment, passion, and drive to succeed?[17]

I believe that it is well worth going through these steps in an honest way. Sometimes, the answer will be *'no'* to the opportunity or *'no'* until a different time. But, hopefully, you have assessed your idea and are even more convinced that it is an excellent opportunity to grasp with both hands.

🚀 🚀 🚀

Action Points:

Checklist

1. Have you considered the market size?
2. Have you considered cash flow?
3. Do you/colleagues have the skills required?
4. Do you and colleagues have commitment/passion?

DEFINE A SMART GOAL

"You can achieve amazing progress if you set a clear goal and find a measure that will drive progress toward that goal."

— BILL GATES, MICROSOFT

Setting goals for your consulting business is essential, as they will help to motivate you and give you a sense of direction.

The **SMART** method in setting goals helps structure your work based on the goals you want to reach and will ensure that your goals are SMART, an acronym that stands for *Specific, Measurable, Achievable, Realistic, and Timely.*

Specific – this means it is clear. You can clarify your specific goal by asking the five **Ws**. *Who will do the goal? What do you want to accomplish? Where will it be achieved? When do you want to achieve the goal? Why do you want to achieve it?*

Measurable – this means you can measure your progress towards achieving the goal.

Achievable – this means it is not impossible.

Realistic - this means that you can get to the goal realistically.

Timely - and time means you have a timeline of when you'll start and achieve it. This should spur you on to action and prevent failure. They will push you and help to organize yourself[18].

ℒ ℒ ℒ

Action Point:

- Set a SMART goal for your consulting business now. You could use the table below to ensure that the goal is SMART.

1. Specific

Example: I want to *set up a consulting business in London by December helping other businesses to free up their time for strategy/development/innovation, by using Virtual PAs, to ultimately grow and develop their business.*

2. Measurable

Example: *Plan to measure the number of businesses that do this? Measure how many hours of PA work they utilize for admin/research/finance/HR – these hours are time saved, allowing them to focus on other aspects of the business – strategy, development etc. Measure their profits over time after using PAs.*

3. Achievable

Example: This seems realistic and achievable. I will consider I have achieved this when I have 6 companies utilizing PAs successfully.

4. Realistic

Example: *This seems realistic – I will aim to get one new business per month. I can commit to this*

5. Timely

Example: *I will start this on the 1st of June and hope to have got 6 businesses on board, by the deadline of the 1st of December.*

DEFINE VALUE PROPOSITION AND MISSION

What does your consulting business do? Whom does it serve, and how does your service set itself apart from the competition? What is your purpose? You need to ask yourself these fundamental questions in the early stages and address them quickly and effectively; otherwise, your target audience will move to the next competitive option, which nowadays is just a click away. The best way to address these questions and ensure you can catch your target audience's attention is by developing a solid value proposition and mission statement.

Sami Inkinen, the Co-founder of Virtua Health, says:

> *"starting a company extracts so much energy and conviction that not having a clear-cut goal and meaningful mission can hamper your success. This is why, at Virta, our mission was clearly defined: reverse early type-2 diabetes in 100 million people by 2025."*[19]

Value proposition

A value proposition is a promise of the value/benefits that you will deliver to your customers. The more specific you can be about this, the more you can charge for your business consulting services. If you can prove that you have helped eight companies reach 6-figures in half a year, it is acceptable to charge more than someone who claims to increase the profitability of companies.[20]

When you create a value proposition, you need to do it simply with clarity; that shows what value you offer to your customer. You must make the best of your team's skills and ensure you're aligned.[21] It's a balance between knowing your customer profile and showing the value you add to create a perfect solution, or what Osterwalder describes as a *'fit'* for them when their problem and your solution meet and fit together like jigsaw pieces[22].

Your value proposition can be broken down into three parts:

1. What products or services do you offer?
2. What pain point will these relieve?
3. What gain/reward is created as a result?[23]

Practical example
Slack's value proposition is a great example:

"Slack is a place where your team comes together to collaborate, important information can be found by the right people, and your tools pipe in information when and where you need it."[24]

To break this down into the three parts mentioned above:

1. The product/service that Slack offers is a *'place' (online)*.
2. The pain point that Slack relieves is that customers need an online space to collaborate with people potentially all over the world. It needs to be a place where they can share information, but it needs to be secure, so only the *'right'* people can access this. This online space must be accessible at all times and anywhere in the world. Because people can read a back-thread, they can catch up on a situation/conversation that occurred earlier.
3. They offer an online safe, secure space where people can collaborate without needing physical space *(that they have to travel to)*. The system can be tailored to people's needs with additional tools.

Mission statement

When it comes to defining your Mission Statement, this is something that explains what your business is about, its objectives, and its approach. You may need to consider your company's culture and commitment to customers and ensure that you can measure, act, and achieve your objectives. This is important, even when you are the only employee starting your own business. Write and communicate your mission statement clearly with clarity. Your mission statement should guide your company and employees, be ethical, and inspire yourself and your staff to work towards common goals. It should make customers, and potential partners/collaborators want to support you.[25]

. . .

Often, companies we connect with and feel we want to support have a mission we believe in. Sometimes mission statements are combined with a vision statement, which you aspire to be.[26] Your mission statement genuinely needs to guide your business and not be just meaningless words you think you should have. You can consider goals, ethics, culture, and how you will make decisions as part of your mission statement. With your mission statement, let people know of the good things you do to help customers. Always ensure your mission statement is accurate and not just using what you think are the politically correct things to say or the buzzwords of the moment.

Practical example

Some examples of mission statements I got motivated by include Patagonia and Tesla because they exemplify what it means to be purpose-driven and stand up for matters they care about while making this the center of their business. Patagonia's mission statement claims, *"We're in business to save our home planet"*, which demonstrates Patagonia's commitment to the environment and to use products that can be recycled and not be detrimental to the environment. Tesla's mission is *"To accelerate the world's transition to sustainable energy."* 'Accelerate' gives the impression of fast cars, yet the mission statement shows a change to how people acquire and use energy in the future. With this mission statement, Tesla wants to convey that it is keen to help people with this transition[27].

🖋 🖋 🖋

Action Points:

- Write down your value proposition and mission statement in the boxes below

I. **Value Proposition**

Example: I can create online SEO content that will drive more people to your website. I have helped 20 companies to increase their online traffic by 10%.

2. Mission Statement:

Example: "The mission of Southwest Airlines is dedication to the highest quality of customer service delivered with a sense of warmth, friendliness, individual pride and company spirit." [28]

CONCRETE PRO TIPS FROM EXPERTS

1. The crucial piece of advice from **Peep Lana** regarding creating a unique value proposition is that you should *"test your value proposition."* By testing it, you need to ensure it is 'relevant' and will show customers how it will solve their issues. It must have a *'quantified value'* and deliver specific consumer advantages. Finally, it needs to have *'differentiation'* that tells customers why people should purchase your services rather than the competition, and it should be specific and easy to understand.[29]

2. **Salesforce** recommends that you learn about their characteristics

and business challenges when trying to identify your customers. Your customers are your advocates for a higher lead-to-close ratio, a shorter sales cycle, and a more significant number of wins/success stories.[30]

3. Peep Laja suggests that value propositions should not be meaningless and full of jargon. They also should not be a slogan or catchphrase. They should avoid hype.[31]

4. *"Starting a company extracts so much energy and conviction that not having a clear-cut goal and meaningful mission can hamper your success."* — **Sami Inkinen**, Co-founder of Virta Health.

5. *"If your goal is to make the world a better place, one thing you can do is pick a specific challenge that you care about. Then, learn as much as you can about it and try to volunteer your time to help an organization that is working in this area. While you're doing that, look for creative new ways to use technology to tackle parts of the problem that you come in contact with."* - **Bill Gates.**

The next chapter will help you to navigate all the legal stuff you should consider when starting a company. It will discuss the type of business you decide to be, whether you start your business on your own or with a partner, dealing with accounting and taxes, and administrative support.

KEY TAKEAWAYS FROM THIS CHAPTER

1. Become focused on your strengths/expertise/what you can offer. Is there something people regularly ask you to help with that you can develop into a consulting business?

2. Understand your audience and their pain points. Is their pain point connected to cost, time, a complicated procedure, or lack of support?

3. Comprehend the industry, the competition, and your competitive advantage. Conduct thorough market research with focus groups, surveys, and press releases before designing products to gauge interest and refine products/services accordingly.

4. Carefully consider whether your business plan is a worthwhile opportunity. Think about the market, sustainability, skills, and commitment when assessing the risk and if the business is viable.

5. Develop SMART goals. Keeping objectives specific, measurable, achievable, realistic, and time goals makes it far more likely that you will achieve them because they are logical, planned, and well-considered as to the steps you will take to complete them.

6. Include a value proposition and meaningful mission statement. Having a value proposition gives you a clear idea of what promises you can secure for your customers. Having a mission statement gives you a constant overarching guide for your business that will steer you *(and your staff)* and keep you accurate to your goals and aims for the company.

3

COMPANY CREATION 101: LEGAL STUFF YOU SHOULD CONSIDER

"The keys to success are patience, persistence, and obsessive attention to detail."

— JEFF BEZOS, AMAZON

The third step to starting and growing your consulting business is dealing with the legal aspects. The content in this chapter will raise your awareness about lawful things you should consider. **However, you should contact a legal counselor and get tax advice before making any decisions impacting your business.**

Many people dream and aspire to run their businesses. But for a company to get fully off the ground and achieve success, it does require more than dreams and aspirations; it needs a lot of planning and organization. You may wish to run a business from a spare room in your house or hope that an angel investor will take you under their wings; regardless of your approach, it is necessary to have a solid business plan. Therefore, this chapter will help you to create a business model and identify the type of business entity that meets your needs. The chapter will cover legal and administrative advice.

<u>By the end of this chapter, you will:</u>

1. Know what business model you wish to take.
2. Be able to define the type of business entity that suits your needs.
3. Assess whether you will work alone or with a partner and fully understand the pros and cons of both options.
4. Think about the administration and other resources required when creating a company.
5. Have helpful tips on dos and don'ts based on others' experiences.

DETERMINE YOUR BUSINESS MODEL

There are several business models, and people have varying definitions of what constitutes one. **A business model** is the main idea of how your business will make money, whereas the business plan goes into more detail.

Essentially a business model should be about what problem you will solve for your customer, how you will do that, and what growth opportunities there are in the market. By having a business model, you are steering the direction the business will head in.[1] Choosing your business model is about choosing how you will add value to people and how you will make your money. I reported some examples below to give you an idea about different business models:

- **Freemium** – where you provide a free product but then charge for add-ons/features.
- **Free trial** – you offer a free trial for a set amount of time, but then customers need to pay if they want this in the future.

- **Licensing** – you can sell licenses to allow people to have permission to use products
- **Open-source** – your product is free, but you may gain money through crowdsourcing.
- **Subscription** – people pay a recurring fee to access the service.[2]

Other models include:

- **Product/Service** – you may make or sell your product or service.
- **Reseller** – You may find products or brands *(that you have not made yourself)* and sell these at a higher price than you acquired the product. Affiliate marketers come under this heading, as do eCommerce companies.
- **Broker** – This person brings a buyer and seller together and takes a transaction fee. A real estate agent is a perfect example of this. PayPal is another, and its role is the exchange of money.[3]
- **Aggregator** – This is a business model where you build a community, then charge for access to the community. Publications and news sites fit into this business model, often based on subscriptions. Shopzilla and Woot are examples of this.[4]

Once you have chosen a business model that suits you, the next thing to do is create a business plan.

DETERMINE YOUR BUSINESS PLAN

You can start by writing a business plan to state your business' purpose. A business plan will enable you to address the following questions: to whom will you be selling? What are your SMART goals? How will you finance startup costs? While this may sound a little unusual when you're excited about starting a new business, it can be sensible to think about an *'exit strategy'* for your business from the start. How will you leave the company when you're ready? Having a business plan will give you an aim and direction, it will highlight any potential difficulties, and it will consider sustainability.[5]

The next chapter of this book looks in much more detail at how you will finance your business, which may feed into your business plan. Additionally, it is essential to remember that your business plan is a work in progress that you will constantly refer to, revisit, and check your progress against.

Having a business plan can be the thing that sets you apart from businesses that fail. To be successful requires you to have a good plan. You need to be able to formulate and execute your plan.

I know it is sometimes hard to know where to start from. I have collected a couple of good online addresses where you can find some examples of business plan templates. When you start, do not waste your time trying to land the best, bulletproof business plan. Just get started and put in as much information as you can. If there is something that you are unsure about, leave it blank and revisit it at a later time. See some options below.

You can get a free business plan template via StartupDaddy in a Word or Excel document. Depending on where you are based in the world, it's worth doing a Google search for a 'free business plan template' and choosing the most reputable source for the area you live in. On websites, you can find business plan templates you can download for free. Sometimes you will find free templates connected to law firms or universities – find one that suits you!

In the USA, there is the U.S. Small Business Administration site that has business plan examples. In the UK, government websites offer a free business plan template.

There are various reasons why you may need to write a business plan. It could be for yourself; it could be to attract partners, or it could be to get investors for your business. Your business plan should include:

- **Executive Summary** – your objectives, mission, keys to success *(up to 2 pages)*.
- **Company Summary** – the ownership, the company location, what the company looks like.
- **Products and or Services**
- **Market Analysis** – segmentation, target markets, needs, trends, growth, industry analysis, main competitors.
- **Strategy and Implementation Plan** – the value proposition, competitive edge, marketing strategy, where you will position yourself, pricing strategy, promotions, sales strategy, forecasting, milestones, when you will make breakthroughs along the way.
- **Management** – the organizational structure and the management, the team, the different roles.
- **Financial plan** – break-even analysis, profit, loss, cash flow statement, and balance sheet.
- **Appendix** – supporting documents, research, reference material.[6]

A business plan is a good starting point, but a business model also needs to map out how you will continue to create value for your customers in the future. You need to know how you'll start, how it will progress, how you will monitor your success levels, and how you will create value.

It is also essential to consider how your business plans will interact with others in the industry. A good business plan will create a cycle that will give you a competitive advantage over time.

🕮 🕮 🕮

Action Points:

1. Having read the above. Take some time to think about the best Business Model for your business.
2. Start to devise a business plan – which can be a work in progress and constantly revised and updated.

DETERMINE AND CREATE YOUR LEGAL BUSINESS STRUCTURE (DEFINE THE TYPE OF BUSINESS ENTITY)

There are various legal business structures. Clearly speaking, it means how your company is organized and how laws govern its operations. Selecting the right one for your needs is crucial because it will impact your business' finances, the taxes you pay, and the liability you face should anything happen to the business. It is essential for you to choose a legal structure before you can register your company.

For example, in America, you must register with the Secretary of State's office of the business location. In the UK, you can register your business with the HMRC and Companies House.

The following chapter will give you general guidance, but you should contact the sector's relevant professionals. Let's now take a look at the four fundamental types of business entity so that you can decide which suits you best:

1. Sole proprietorship

This is where you own the business, and therefore you are personally responsible for debts and obligations. This route could impact your credit if the company does not go well. If you have a sole proprietorship, you can't offer stocks *(this is only for corporations)*, which may make it harder to fundraise. With a sole proprietorship, you don't have partners or executive boards. It is easy to end, and you can dissolve your business at any point. Perhaps it is interesting to note that several famous companies started as sole proprietors, including eBay, JCPenney, Walmart, and Marriott Hotels![7]

2. A Partnership

This is where two or more people are liable for the business. You would share profits and losses in a partnership and make decisions together. Ideally, you should get an attorney to review a partnership agreement. Getting a business loan with more than one owner can be more manageable. For instance, Google started as a partnership between Larry Page and Sergey Brin. Other very successful partnerships have included: Warner Bros., Ben and Jerry's, Apple, Twitter, Microsoft, and Hewlett-Packard.[8]

3. A Corporation

There are different types of a corporation *(C, S, or B)*, but by having a corporation structure, the business exists as a separate entity from its owners. **C corporations,** such as Amazon, Apple, and Bank of America, are owned by shareholders. **S corporations** are for small businesses. **B corporations** are benefit corporations for corporate social responsibility businesses that positively impact society. With a corporation, a person is shielded from personal liability for business debts. So, potentially, in a worst-case scenario, the business would become bankrupt, but not the actual person. A corporation can own property, assume liability, pay taxes, enter contracts, and sue, as an individual can. If you intend to get funding, this can be a sensible option. If you have a corporation, you need to put in place a hierarchy with a board of directors who must meet so many times a year. A ranking can prevent a company from closing if a partner transfers shares, exits, or dies.

4. Limited Liability Company

this is the most common type of business structure for small businesses; because they have protections that a corporation offers but the tax benefits of a partnership. Small businesses can be LLCs, but also many larger businesses take this structure, such as

Anheuser-Busch, Pepsi-Cola, Sony, IBM, Nike, and Hertz Rent-a-Car.[9]

When I first started, I hesitated between having a Corporation or a Limited Liability Company. Here are some of the most relevant findings to help you with the decision:

LLC	Corporation
Both of these options limit your liability and give some separation between the business and you as a person	
• has articles of organization and an operating agreement	• is formed when articles of incorporation documents are completed + a board of directors needs to oversee the business.
• members have an ownership interest in the business assets because they've invested in joining the company	• owners are shareholders who have shares of stock in the business.
• owners deal with any profits or losses directly	• the corporation pays income tax on gains or losses, not the owners • some dividends may be paid to owners, but the corporation can keep earnings too
• members pay tax on their tax returns; they are classed as self-employed	• taxed at 21%. Shareholders also pay tax on their dividends

Action Point:

- Considering the various business structures, which do you think is most suited for your business type? **Write it in the box below:**

Example: As a small growing business, with only myself as a staff member, I opted for sole proprietorship. However, as the business expands and I start to employ people, I may consider changing the business to a Limited Liability Company.

ASSESS WHAT IS THE BEST OPTION (WHETHER TO START ALONE OR WITH A PARTNER)

Consider whether you want to start a business yourself. Or with a partner/s.

There are pros and cons to both. The pros of starting a business are that you can make all the decisions without needing to consult anyone else. You can run the business exactly how you want to, with no discussions/arguments. You can steer the company in the direction you want. You have sole control. When the business is successful, you have the pleasure of knowing this is all down to you and your hard work, which is enormously satisfying and rewarding, with a sense of pride and achievement.

It is easy to set up a sole proprietorship. The business is you; you are the business. There's not as much paperwork or red tape, it's not expensive, you can easily dissolve the company should you want to, you will get all the profits and losses. When you start a business on your own, it does allow you to work and do your new business part-time until you get to a point where you can do the business full-time.

There is a famous quote by Steve Jobs, where he said:

"One person never does great things in business; a team of people does them."

The cons of starting a business on your own are that you don't have anyone to bounce ideas off *(unless you have supportive friends/family/network around you)*. You don't have anyone to challenge whether your ideas are sensible or risky or to provide an alternative viewpoint. Starting a business can be pretty isolating, and you must invest time and energy. If you're doing this alone, it can take a physical and emotional toll on one's health.

If you set up a sole proprietorship, you are personally liable for any debt incurred by the business. It is more challenging to raise capital independently; you can only do so much as one person *(admin, marketing, billing, etc.)*. Sole proprietors do not get some of the tax benefits that corporations are entitled to. Once you die, the business ceases to exist.

The pros of starting a business with a partner are that you have support in all business areas. You will bring different strengths, skills, and experience to strengthen the company. You may achieve a more outstanding balance with the two-heads-are-better-than-one approach. You are more likely to get a business loan with two people *(or more)* rather than just one to help finance the business.

You can share the responsibility, roles, and stress. You have someone to bounce ideas off. You can motivate one another to strive for your goals. You have someone to be accountable to, which can keep the business focused and organized.

Some advice on how to choose your business partner includes implicit trust. If you don't trust them with your bank account, then don't go into partnership with them.

Are their goals, values, and responsibilities aligned with yours? Consider a *'trial run'* before you enter into a partnership. Don't let someone become a partner if they'd be better off as a consultant.

Ensure you and your partner have different strengths. Be clear about each of your responsibilities and ensure these are balanced relatively.

Have firm agreements about funding and profit sharing before the partnership. Have a value for the company so that if one partner leaves, the buy/sell agreements are in place and clear.

You want a partner who is as enthusiastic and committed as you. It's good to have a partner who is easy to communicate with. You don't want to feel constantly battling against someone reluctant, combative, or who can't see your point of view. You don't want someone dealing with a challenging life *(and therefore doesn't have time to focus on the business)*. If your partner has resources and credibility, this is beneficial. Your partner should be financially stable. Ensure they have qualities of honesty and good business ethics. And finally, you should respect one another.

The cons of starting a business with a partner are that you may have differences of opinion as to how the company should run. Despite trying to split work equally, it could be that one partner ends up doing more work than the other, and this can cause resentment.

Decisions can take longer because you both *(or more people if there are more than just two partners)* have to be consulted. If one partner wishes to move on from the business, this can cause some issues *(this is why it's important to get contracts drawn up at the start and have an attorney check them)*. You and your partners will be liable for any debts against the business. If your partner dies, you could also terminate the company.

ᖯ ᖯ ᖯ

Action Point:

- Take some time to **write a list** of the specific pros and cons as to whether you'd instead start a business on your own or with a partner/s.

It is worth also considering that if you start a business as a sole proprietor, you could always enlist the help of *'associates'* who work for you on a self-employed basis as and when required.

They are responsible for paying their taxes, and you're hiring them for freelance work, which can be short-term or long-term. With time and the development of the business, it is possible to change the legal business structure.

You can switch to a more complex system, for example, moving from a sole proprietorship to a corporation. You may wish to do this to lessen your liability or for tax considerations. It could be due to increasing employees, a change in ownership, etc. If you want to change your business structure, it is ALWAYS worth getting an attorney and tax professional involved to ensure everything is adequately covered.

ACCOUNTING

Once you have decided what your legal business structure will be, you need to register your business with the government and IRS *(Inland Revenue Service – which deals with tax in America)*. If you are in the US, you may need to complete various business licenses with federal, State, and local governments. **In America, you need to:**

1. Choose your State.
2. Name your company.
3. Hire a Registered Agent Service.
4. File your LLC *(if this is the company you have chosen)* with the State.
5. Create an LLC Operating Agreement.
6. Get an EIN.

7. Have a physical US mailing address.
8. Open a US Bank Account.
9. Prepare for US tax filing.

Registering your business with the HMRC (Her Majesty's Revenue and Customs – who collect taxes) as a sole trader is sufficient in the UK. Still, if you're a limited company, you need to register with Companies House, and if you need to register for VAT if you have an income of £85,000 per year in the UK.

In America, to set up a company and deal with your accounting and taxes, you may need to do the following things:

1. Complete an *'articles of incorporation document'* which gives the business name, purpose, corporate structure, stock details, and other information about your company.

2. If you have an LLC, you may need an *'operating agreement',* a contract between the LLC members listing details of the organization's ownership, structure, and finances.

3. If you don't have articles of incorporation or an operating agreement, you will still need to register your business name; this is the name you are Doing Business As *(DBA)*. You can get DBA certificates and may need to pay a registration fee. You may also want to trademark your business name.

4. If you have employees, you may need an Employer Identification Number for them from the IRS.

5. You will need to pay taxes depending on your chosen business structure and where you live in the world. You may need a local business license or seller's permit. So be sure to do the proper due diligence before setting up your business.

6. It is sensible too to get insurance for your business for damage, theft, liability, etc.

7. You will need to consider how much to pay yourself from the business earnings. It needs to be reasonable and increased over time when the business becomes more successful. Also, consider retirement plans right from the offset; it's sensible to plan for the future and reduce your tax too.

TAXES

If you have a small business and are a sole proprietorship or LLC, you will need to estimate tax payments quarterly and pay tax to a government or State, depending on where you live. It is essential to pay tax on time because you will receive a penalty fine if they are late, and this may increase depending on how many days late the tax is. It is advisable to put away at least 1/3 of any income earned for taxes.

Employees

If you have employees on a payroll, your business will have W-2 income, and you will be required to deduct the tax from each employee's salary and send the tax to the government. Your responsibility is to pay the correct amount, but it is worth getting a trusted accountant to check this for you. You will also have to consider the costs of hiring an accountant to help you.

Bank account and savings

It is advisable to set up a separate business bank account, different from your bank account, so it's easy to keep money separated. You may wish to set up a business credit card too. If you need to charge sales tax, you may need software to keep track of this. Learn about what is or isn't tax deductible so that you are not paying more tax than you need to.

Track your business expenses and consider setting up a retirement plan and health savings account for your business *(these may have some tax advantages)*.

🖋 🖋 🖋

Action Points:

- Do some online research for the country you live in to find out whom you need to register your business with *(also dependent upon your business structure)*. **Write what you found in the box below:**

Example: As a sole trader in the UK, I need to register my business with HMRC. If I change to become a limited company, I need to register with Companies House, and register for VAT once my income reaches £85,000 per year.

- Make a note of what documents your business structure requires? Do you need an operating agreement for an LLC? Do you need an article of incorporation document? If so, your next step could be to search for free *'template'* documents for these online; there are plenty to choose from. However, it's always sensible to seek proper legal advice to ensure everything adheres to rules, laws, and legislation rather than coming unstuck further down the line.

Checklist (only do what is needed for your type of business)

1. Operating agreement?
2. Articles of incorporation?
3. Template documents?
4. Register DBA?
5. Trademark your business?
6. Get EIN numbers?
7. Ensure you pay taxes?
8. Local business license/permit?
9. Insurance?
10. Separate business bank account?
11. Hire an accountant?

ADMINISTRATIVE SUPPORT AND RESOURCES

As mentioned above in the cons of being a sole proprietor section, one person can only do some much with the time they have available in a day. If you're a sole proprietor, it's tough to juggle administrative tasks, marketing, generating new customers, billing, accounts, taxes, creating the product, or providing the service you wish to offer.

As your business becomes busier, you may wish to get some administrative support and other employees to assist with your essential service, plus things like marketing, finance, and HR. When you start to take on board employees, it's sensible to write a list of all tasks that need to be done and then work out which YOU have to do; and what could be done by someone else. These tasks, which someone else could do, can form the basis of a job description.

℘ ℘ ℘

Action Points:

- Can you manage to do all the jobs you need to do currently? If so, it's still worth considering that if you had someone doing the more mundane administrative tasks, what would free up more of your time to do *(strategy, development)* that could grow or improve the business?

- Consider what other resources would help your business run smoothly. Can you acquire or hire these resources?

CONCRETE PRO TIPS FROM EXPERTS

1. Think about your business' legal structure before setting it up. It's better to get this right the first time so that you can register it with the correct places, pay the correct tax, complete the proper documents, and have the correct liability cover. While you can change your business structure in the future, it can be a little complicated and have consequences on your taxes. Also, if you forget any essential step while doing so, your business could be dissolved.

2. Build a team of trusted experts – lawyers, accountants, tax and financial advisers, marketing team, etc.

3. Take some time to think carefully about structure. Don't make hasty or *'easy'* decisions when starting your business structure. It is easier to create a sole proprietorship or partnership. But they lack liability protection. It may take longer to complete a corporation, but it would give you liability protection and potentially better tax options.

The next chapter will take a detailed look at how to finance your business while you're still building it. It will discuss the importance of reinvesting money in your business to grow and develop it and will contain helpful expert tips of *'dos'* for success and *'don'ts'* to help you avoid mistakes others have made. I will assist you in determining your costs and give you various options on how you could sponsor them.

KEY TAKEAWAYS FROM THIS CHAPTER

1. A business model is about how the business will work. What is the value proposition? How will the business grow? How will the company make money? Your business model should give a direction for the industry, highlight any difficulties, and look at sustainability. It should be about the choices you have made as a business owner. Your business model will be a work in progress.

2. Think carefully about what business structure suits you? Sole proprietorship, partnership, corporation, or LLC?

3. Ensure your business is registered with whom it needs to be and any documents completed, such as an *'articles of incorporation'*, VAT, an operating agreement, DBA, EIN, insurance, and retirement plans, and remember to pay taxes for your business and your employee's wages. Set up a separate business bank account.

4. Take on support for administrative tasks and other employee resources where needed to free up more time for you to make strategic business decisions that will grow the business.

4

MONEY TALKS – HOW TO FINANCE YOUR BUSINESS

The fourth step to starting and growing your own consulting business from zero is to be able to finance it. Your area of expertise will bring in finance, but you need to manage this well. While some of the concepts here may seem obvious, many entrepreneurs overlook the importance of considering their finances seriously and fail to have a solid plan. The phrase *"fail to prepare, prepare to fail"* is very accurate in this case, as many businesses sadly fail due to poor financial management. Starting on an excellent financial footing with your business is vital to cover short-term costs, and longer-term development needs to grow the business.

Have you considered how much money your business will need and where you will find it? Have you thought about what you will pay yourself? Have you considered reviewing your finances regularly and keeping them in check to have good future credit?[1]

By the end of this chapter, you will:

1. Have a good concept of how to manage your money and finances while you are growing your own consulting business from zero.
2. Determine your costs – this chapter will cover all the obvious costs and some hidden costs you may not have anticipated.
3. Be informed about what options could finance your business and have a good idea of which is the best option/s for you.
4. Know how you can reinvest in your business.
5. Know some good advice to follow from experts, and some don'ts to avoid the pitfalls.

MONEY MANAGEMENT AND HOW TO FINANCE YOUR BUSINESS WHILE BUILDING IT

Money management is how you manage the cash flow in and out of your business. It includes budgeting, saving, investing, spending, income, and expenditure, and ensuring you know at all times your financial situation.[2]

I've seen numerous businesses fail because of poor money management. Especially when you launch a new venture, expenditures are going to be more significant than income, which requires some planning.

In my experience, I started my business on the side while I was still working in a corporation. I've heard a lot of different opinions about this. People told me that if I was not quitting my job, I was not committed enough to my business, and consequently, it would never take off. Unfortunately, I don't know you personally, so I can't tell you what will work for you. What I can tell you is that the fact of not quitting my corporate job while I was building my company allowed me to have the mental space and tranquility to give my business my best version. As I explained in Chapter 1, it came with many sacrifices, but finances were never keeping me up at night.

How much do you need to start your business?

Many suggest that you require six months of savings to start a business in order to cover your costs and expenses during that time. Some others suggest you need a year, but this high amount could discourage you from starting your business.

What may be reassuring to know is that, on average, business startups typically cost less than $10,000. These figures are moderate and are not industry-specific. They also don't differentiate between a business in an office/shop location and a home-based business.[3]

There are some other options, though, to make the financing of your own consulting business slightly smoother. Rather than just leaping full-time into a new consulting firm, you could work part-time or full-time employment. Start by doing business consulting in your spare time or part-time until you feel you have built up enough of a reputation and client base to transition to this being your full-time career.

The ROI

When you look at your finances, which it is sensible to take time to do each month, keep a check on Return on Investment *(ROI)*. When you look at expenditure, consider that what you have spent is paying off and bringing you rewards. You could create an income and expenditure spreadsheet in Excel to keep track of your finances each month. You will presumably have a specific business account, and you can view this online to see income and expenditure *(Money In and Money Out)*. Many software packages can help you keep track of accounts or invoices, such as QuickBooks, SquareUp, Xero, Fresh-Books, and Waive. You can ensure that you have a hard-copy or electronic file where you keep copies of any purchase orders, receipts, and invoices.[4]

🐾 🐾 🐾

Action Points:

- Think about what options are best for you. Do you think you will try to save up at least 6-12 months of expenses? Are you willing to quit some nights at the pub/clubs, buy the latest computer game system, or get parts for your car and start saving and investing that money into building a business? Do you have the savings already to invest?
- Would working part-time in your consulting business be a viable option for you? Until it gains traction and customers?
- Or, do you want to immerse yourself in the world of consulting right away entirely and will seek funding elsewhere *(see later in this chapter for options on how to finance your business)*?

DETERMINE YOUR COSTS

The costs you will incur when building a consulting business from zero will include upfront costs of creating a business plan, research expenses, borrowing costs, technology, advertising, promotion, and employee expenses, and filing costs if you set up a partnership or corporation.[5]

Many good business ideas have failed because people have started and run out of resources. If people had planned better, this might not have been the case. People should ask for larger loans initially; rather than run out of money and fall into bad credit, where you cannot get any more funds due to the bad credit.[6] To plan, you can make some lists. You'll have to do some *'estimating'* and then add up the costs. If you're unsure of expenses, to be as realistic as possible, do some online research to find out.[7] My advice would be to always overestimate costs rather than underestimate.

The steps below will give you some starting points to springboard your thoughts on determining the costs of starting your consulting business:

Step 1 – What do you predict your sales will be each month for providing the service of your consulting business? If unsure, you may need more contingency funds than you expect.

Step 2 – What do you predict your expenditure will be each month? You need to know how much money you need each month while your business starts to cover costs and expenses. You can break costs into *'pre-opening'* and *'post-opening'* startup costs. *'Pre-opening'* costs refer to the expenses incurred in the business plan, research, borrowing costs, and fees for IT. In contrast, *'post-opening'* startup costs refer to advertising, promotion, employees, etc.

If for example, you plan to hire people to do market research for you, it would be sensible to gain three quotes from different firms and then go with the firm that offers you the best deal *(not necessarily the cheapest)*.[8] You will have one-time costs, then monthly expenses that will reoccur, and it's a good idea to know what you can expect for both. It's also wise to factor in some additional money for unexpected or overlooked expenses because there will undoubtedly be some. It's sensible advice to chat with as many people as possible who have set up similar businesses to share best practices and learn from those who have already gone through this *'struggle'*.

Step 3 – What other costs/expenses may occur? What equipment do you need to purchase? Are there monthly subscription expenses for software packages? MS Word? Grammarly? Accounting *(professional fees)*/Payroll?[9] Remember that if you need to purchase equipment, keep a note of this for your tax return, *i.e.*, if you need a new work computer, printer, etc.

You may need to consider insurance *(liability, errors and omissions, business interruption, home-based business)* and supplies as part of your costs. Will you need to hire any consultants for your business? Will you need to travel to meetings with companies in person? If so, include travel expenses when you're doing your costing.[10]

In an article by Profitable Venture, they put forth the following estimated cost breakdown for starting a consulting business in 2022:

1. The Total Fee for incorporating the business: **$750**
2. The budget for Liability insurance, permits, and license: **$2,500**
3. The Amount needed to acquire a suitable Office facility in a business district for six months *(Re-Construction of the facility inclusive)*: **$40,000**
4. The Cost for equipping the office *(computers, printers, fax machines, furniture, telephones, filing cabins, safety gadgets, and electronics)*: **$2,000**
5. The Cost of Launching your official Website: **$600**
6. Budget for paying at least two employees for three months and utility bills: **$10,000**
7. Additional Expenditure *(Business cards, Signage, Adverts, and Promotions)*: **$2,500**
8. Miscellaneous: **$1,000**[11]

Plan for the worst

Looking at your income, expenditure, and other costs will help you to prepare a budget and cash flow forecast. Be realistic and ever so slightly *'pessimistic'* in your predictions – this is to account for *'risk'* and have some *'buffer'* or *'runway'* if things don't go to plan. This isn't to be overly negative, and if you achieve more than your predictions, fantastic. But it's better to underestimate income and overestimate expenditure rather than have a nasty surprise if something doesn't go to plan or something unexpected crops up *(for example, your biggest client leaves)*.[12]

Be humble

It's also wise to be modest with your expenditure as you grow your business. Jeff Bezos once commented that when people congratulate him after a quarterly earnings announcement, he says: *"Thank you, but that quarter was baked three years ago"*, meaning that he was super organized and prepared and always thinking ahead for the future. Another example from Jeff Bezos is when he says: *"It's hard to remember for your guys, but for me, it's like yesterday I was driving the packages to the post office myself and hoping one day we could afford a forklift."* This shows that he started from humble origins of zero and didn't overspend money he didn't have initially but built up to bigger and better things with time.[13]

Hard work will pay off

It can be typical for startup businesses to have higher expenditure than income for the first two or three years while they establish themselves. Do not let this get you down because the hard work will pay off, and it will be worth it if you are patient. But this is something to be aware of and keep in mind initially. Generally, in the first year of running a business, a person would take a salary of less than their previous income and ideally invest most profits into the company. You may draw your previous salary in the second year, and you can attract more significant wages in future years.[14]

Seasonality

Depending on the season, your business could have peaks and troughs; sometimes, during extensive holiday periods in your country, work may ease off as people focus on spending time with their family and celebrating rather than work. Hence, it would be best if you prepared for these times of less work/income.[15]

Start from home

Typically, people who start a consulting business may either do this from home or may rent an office at a business incubation center. Starting a business from home lowers the financial need for office rent, furniture, and bills. Most people who start a business from home will self-finance the company by saving enough money to allow the business to find its feet. This technique cuts down on financial risk and will enable you to become established, gain a reputation, and gain some income.

❦ ❦ ❦

Action Points:

- Have a go at filling out the boxes below to give you some insight into determining your costs:

1. **Expenditure: What will the costs and expenses be per month?** *(Remember you may have start-up costs too, that won't occur every month, but just for when you start your business — paperwork/legal contracts).* **Do you have employees' salaries?**
Example: $750 rent; $740 bills; $245 legal costs; $1,000 to register startup (it can range between $600 to $1400 depending on the state) It may cost more for a partnership, or corporation than a sole proprietorship.

```

```

2. **Other costs: subscriptions, equipment, accounting, payroll?**
Example: Adobe and MS subscriptions $35; Accountant:$245; Accounting software: $20

```

```

3. **Add up the expenditure and other Costs, and then deduct the income**

Example: The expenditure here is $3,035 – that's a deficit of $1,035 from the income you bring in, providing everything goes smoothly ... customer's pay on time, there are no hidden extra costs unaccounted for. This is providing you get all the customers you'd expected, and a customer doesn't leave. This deficit and more, needs accounting for when considering startup costs to ensure you have all costs covered. Now initially in the first month – you do have the cost of registering the business, which you wouldn't have in subsequent months. This would reduce the deficit per month moving forward. The IRS allow you to deduct $5,000 if business startup, providing your startup costs are less than $50k.

OPTIONS TO FINANCE YOUR BUSINESS

It is important to give much thought and preparation to finance before you need it. Don't ever wait for things to become urgent before seeking bank loans, overdrafts, credit cards, or funding from other sources.

Do you have money saved or investments you can sell? Investment finance is what businesses typically use, which can cover your startup costs to develop and grow.

It is impossible to guarantee that your business will generate enough profit to pay back the interest on any borrowed money. You 'could' consider taking out a mortgage on a property that you own so that you can use the money towards the business, but then your home is at risk if the company fails and you aren't able to keep up mortgage payments *(so this is a hazardous option)*.

If you decide to invest in your own company, external funders can perceive this positively because they can see you invested in your own company in a genuine and literal way; you have *'skin in the game.'*[16]

Possible sources of finance may include

1. **Yourself** - this is called *'bootstrapping'* and is where you scrape personal funds in your savings account, credit cards, and home equity.[17] Doing this can keep costs low until your business becomes profitable without incurring the debt from interest loans.

2. **Friends and Family** - asking friends and family mean you typically don't end up paying interest on any money borrowed. Jack Ma and his wife started a company in 1995 called China Yellow Pages; five years later, he co-founded Alibaba with 17 friends. This shows the power and success of working with family and friends.[18]

3. **A bank** - this can be a helpful way to scale your business quickly. If you can show that your business has started to gain traction and that a loan would help you, even more, this is often an excellent position.[19]

4. **Other investors** - How much can you, family, and friends afford to invest in the business? People should only invest an amount in the company they can afford to lose. You can let people see your business plan and contemplate it before committing. It's sensible to put any agreements in writing.

Bank Overdrafts and Loans

Your bank will need a business plan with a thorough budget before they offer you a loan. It can be sensible to check your credit score because depending on whether your credit score is good or bad, it may impact what funding you can obtain.

It's reasonable to build a good relationship with your bank and let them know of any changes between figures predicted and achieved and if you have any significant events in the future *(new customers that you think are guaranteed).* If you ever think you will be unable to meet loan payments, or exceed your overdraft, let your bank know immediately.

Short-term?

If you need short-term finance, an overdraft is an excellent option to help you meet the shortfall until you receive customer payments. You may get bank charges and high-interest rates if you exceed your overdraft.

Or, Long-term?

Loans typically are fixed for a set number of years. If you need equipment or vehicles, you may want a loan for these over a long period. Some things such as *'leasing'* or *'hire purchase'* can give you more money than a loan but can cost more too. If you require property, you need to do this via a mortgage. Using your overdraft to finance long-term borrowing is never a good idea because you wouldn't have a short-term finance buffer if required.

Loans vs overdrafts

- Take a look at the table below for more details

Overdrafts	Loans
With overdrafts and loans, you need to know how much interest you will be paying and find the best deal.	
• your bank 'could' ask for repayment of this in full, at any time, typically with just 24 hours' notice	• be mindful of the repayment schedule • If a loan turns you down, you can often go through appeal systems • some loan places allow you to take a 'payment holiday,' which may give your business time for cash flow to generate • banks will want to know you can afford the loan payments and interest and typically will want some security for the loan if you cannot pay
Also it is worth noting that banks will usually only lend up to 50-60% of the value of business property.	

Personal guarantee

You can decide if you want to be a personal guarantee to pay any business debts and use individual assets such as your house *(this is a risky move)*. You are already liable for all business debts if you're a sole trader or a partnership. Typically, Directors of limited companies will provide personal guarantees in case the business fails too. Taking insurance is a good idea so that the loan payments will still be made if you have an accident, become ill, or die.

Don't accumulate debt

It is sensible to pay off all debt funding as soon as possible. Don't let your business credit cards get too high, keep them low; and don't take out loans if you can't afford the repayments.

Grants/Schemes

It's worth checking if you are eligible for any grants or schemes. There could be some available to assist startup or SME businesses.

Often governments will offer some business support organizations, trade associations, or charities aligned with your business ideas. These can often get support if your company exports, technology, or training. Look for a local business development center; these are usually *'incubation'* centers attached to universities, or your local government may have a business growth hub, both of which should be able to provide you with invaluable advice. Your local chamber of commerce is also definitely worth contacting.

Outside Investors?

Are you able to attract any outside investors? Is this the route you want to take for your business? You need to show you have a strong track record and that your business plan is viable to get outside investors interested. Outside investors will usually want a share of your business in return. Their experience could help your business. Investors will typically want an *'exit'* plan too.

Crowdfunding

There are also crowdfunding investors; as the name suggests, crowdfunding is where a large group of people *(a crowd)* invest small amounts in meeting the investment need. There is such a thing as *'loan crowdfunding'* if you can't secure a loan from the bank.

Examples of crowdfunding sites include Kickstarter and Indie-GoGo. It's worth noting that with Kickstarter, you only get to keep the money if you raise the total amount of your goal, but IndieGoGo will let you keep what you raise *(and they take a cut of the proceeds)*. Crowdfunding tends to work more for *'products'* or gadgets than services.[20]

Business Angels

Business Angels are wealthy entrepreneurs who could be willing to invest the equivalent of thousands of dollars. Suppose you've reached a point where you need office space and technology to expand further, and it's more than *'bootstrapping'* or crowdfunding would afford. In that case, you could look to angel investors, already established in the business, who want to invest in promising companies. Online sites, such as Angel Capital Association, and AngelList, help entrepreneurs connect with investors. Angel investors will often provide you with networking opportunities and knowledge or mentorship. If you go for an angel investor, try to select someone aligned with your way of working.[21]

Venture Capital Firms

Venture capital investors may invest one million dollars or more. These will give you the most money, but you will want a perfect business plan. They usually want to invest their client's money into businesses and get a return of 3-10 times what they support within the next 5-7 years.[22] Often you will meet VCs through other entrepreneurs or investors. So, it's always worth networking! A venture capitalist will risk investing in early-stage companies, hoping they'll be profitable. This is usually for companies that have passed the *'seed stage'* and want to grow the company and make it perhaps international.[23]

Jeff Bezos and Jack Ma have both now become venture capitalists and are investing in new companies. Jeff has invested in Business Insider, and the company is using the money to hire more staff and expand the site's subscription research and advertising staff.[24] Jack Ma has a venture capital firm, Yunfeng Capital, which invests in early-stage companies based in China.[25]

ℬ ℬ ℬ

Action Points:

1. Write a list of all the people who could help to finance the business (*yourself, friends, and family*).

2. Set up a business bank account (*sole traders often mix their business and personal finances, it is best to keep these separate!*).
3. Request an overdraft.
4. Request credit cards.
5. Research into any grants/schemes/funders.
6. Look for outside investors.
7. Speak with an accountant regarding finance options – this is really important, often people try to do things themselves and cut-corners, but accountants who are trained in the field, can spot ways to improve cashflow and profitability of the business. It's money well spent.
8. If appropriate ask the bank for a bank loan.

HOW TO REINVEST

Setting aside money is crucial to growing your business and helping it move forward and thrive. You need to be innovative and attract the best employees in the future.[26] Reinvesting money in your business will create a company with more value, rather than just spending the profits on yachts and parties.

Delegate

With time 'reinvesting' profits into the business could mean that you have contractors working for you. This is an excellent return on investment because you can spend 3 hours a day on high-value tasks that will pay for the contractor often. They can spend time on the lower-value functions that have been consuming your time and preventing the business from growing and developing.

If you're unsure of what tasks to delegate to others, write ALL the functions you do in a day, and consider what 'could' be done by others; and what YOU need to do. Look at the tasks that bring in the most income and think how much more these could generate if you had more time to spend on them. Similarly, you could invest money into the business for systems and processes to automate the consulting firm. Anything that makes processes swifter and easier saves you time and leaves you more time to do what you do well.

Invest in training and mentorship

A growth mindset, where you're constantly working towards goals, and acting, will require an investment of time, money, and energy. You may decide to write a book, produce a course, undertake training in new skills, and take on new time members; all of this is investing in your business to grow it further. You could reinvest in your business by paying for time with consultants/experts who have thriving businesses to learn their tips and tricks. Investing money back into your marketing business will give you a good ROI when it generates more customers for your consulting firm.[27]

℘ ℘ ℘

Action Points:

- Take some time to think about how much money you would like to aim to set aside for business growth each month.
- Next, do some *'brainstorming'* to produce ideas about what business development or growth ideas could help your business in the future by investing today. There is a quote by Mahatma Gandhi *"the future depends on what we do in the present."*

CONCRETE PRO TIPS FROM EXPERTS

I. Contact family and friends to see if they can help to finance your business. Jeff Bezos, the CEO of Amazon, had his parents invest $300,000 in Amazon.[28]

2. Look for Angel Investors once your business is thriving but you want to take it to the next level of growth. Jeff Bezos raised $1 million in funding, with 20 investors who spent $50,000 each for a 1% stake.[29]

3. If your company does well, reinvest the money that does social good too. Bill Gates claims that his *'best investment'* turned $10 billion into $200 billion worth of economic benefit. He invested money to increase access to vaccines, which created a 20-to-1 return.[30] Bill Gates also recommends investing in yourself, especially studying *"invest in your education."*[31] So, if your business makes a profit, it's a good idea to reinvest some of the money on gaining more qualifications and skills to help the company further.

4. To plan for the future and to be resilient as a business, you must reinvest in your business. Sundar Pichai, CEO of Alphabet and Google, states, *"We want to be resilient in moments like this. We are very excited about the opportunities ahead. And so, we are investing. We are continuing to hire, bringing in great talent [we] continue investing."*[32]

The next chapter will focus on getting clients and how to build up a customer list fast. It will look at how to create long-term relationships with clients so that you retain them and get more out of them, networking and leveraging existing partnerships.

KEY TAKEAWAYS FROM THIS CHAPTER

1. Consider working part-time while building your business.
2. Invoice swiftly and offer creative options to get people to pay you on time.
3. Split tax bills into monthly installments.
4. Work with an accountant to check your finances monthly.
5. Get a larger loan to finance your company to cover costs, over-estimate rather than under-estimate, and request ALL you need in one go.

6. Work out your expected income, expenditure, and other costs.
7. There are four main types of finance: yourself, friends and family, a bank, or other investors, including grants/loans, angel investors, and crowdfunding.
8. Reinvest in your business to try to make a better future.

5

CLIENT'S FIRST

> *"Selling is not a pushy, winner-takes-all, macho act. It is an empathy-led, process-driven, and knowledge-intensive discipline. Because, in the end, people buy from people."*
>
> — SUBROTO BAGCHI, MINDTREE

The fifth step to starting and growing your own consulting business from zero is to attract clients quickly so that they can benefit from your expertise and bring in income, build your reputation, and grow your successful company. Without clients, you won't have anyone to provide a consulting business to, regardless of your area of expertise.

Your clients are essential; they're the people who will bring in income to the company, which will eventually help it to thrive and grow. I wanted to dedicate an entire chapter to this topic because of how crucial clients are to the success of your business. In the following paragraphs, I will teach you how to gain your very first clients and, notably, how to build long-term relationships with them so that you retain them and gain recommendations and referrals to win other new clients.

By the end of this chapter, you will:

1. Have a good insight into various tips, tricks, and steps you can take to generate leads for new clients.
2. Learn how to gain firm contracts from new clients.
3. Learn skills to build relationships with new clients and how to retain them.
4. Know how to keep your clients long-term.
5. Be able to develop and get more out of your existing clients.
6. Learn various dos and don'ts pro tips from experts.

WIN YOUR FIRST CLIENTS AND BUILD LONG-TERM RELATIONSHIPS

When you're just starting with a new business, clients rarely come flocking to your door immediately. Generally, each new customer you gain is because you've gone out and actively targeted your services to them, you've put yourself and your skills and what your business offers out there. When you're a bit more established, you may get repeat customers, and those customers will recommend you to others. But here, I look at how to get those initial customers.

My advice would be to be patient and to prepare for this to take a little longer than you hoped to build up gradually. This is where your *'runway' (ideally 6-12 months of operating expenses)* that you'll have factored in when thinking about money management and how to determine and finance your costs will be helpful *(see Chapter 4 for a refresher about this)*. Remember that as a brand-new business, your business doesn't currently have an excellent long-standing reputation that is trusted and can be relied upon, so when you start, your credibility is essential.[1] These tips below may help you to win your first clients:

Network with everyone you can!

Talk to everyone you know about your business and what services you offer. It's best to talk in person if possible because you'll make better personal connections than an email would. If you can be involved in a community group – and genuinely involved in them *(not just to be self-serving)*, this may generate business opportunities.

Network with other businesspeople, especially those groups who assist entrepreneurs in growing – there may be business hubs, peer networks, or business breakfasts to attend.[2] It's never too early to network because you can build relations before building your business, during the start-up stage, and at every point throughout your business. People are what will make your business run, and you need these connections, referrals, and recommendations. It is not easy; relationships do not build immediately. They take time for trust to develop, so start developing relationships as soon as possible.

Always behave impeccably in all you do online; when you're out socially, be friendly and helpful with all you meet because you never know if these people will remember you. Suppose you're not a *'people person';* you will need to push yourself to get out there for the sake of your business. You can network online too. There are a couple of sites such as Eventbrite and Meetup.com that may help you to find relevant events happening in your area. Google event search and Lunchclub.com help connect you to people in your area for a phone call. You can enter what you're working on and who you want to meet, and it will connect you to people you can virtually network with.[3]

You can attend industry-related conferences, which are a great place to network. You could also decide to hold your event. It's a great way to network and pitch your services to a group of people in a room. People buy services from people they know and are less bothered about your literature and website. If they meet you and see that you're enthusiastic, passionate, convincing, and credible, they're much more likely to buy into the service you offer.[4]

Collaborate with competitors

Rather than viewing people as enemies or rivals, if you can reach out to competitors, they may either give you surplus work that they're too busy to take. With time, you may work on projects together, and because of your diverse skills, or just because more people are working on it, you may reach more people between you than alone.[5]

You can do this in the early stages of running a business because they may give you work that will help to build your experience. Later in your career, you, too, could help people start the business.

Ensure your online presence is consistent across channels

The content you create for your website and social media must be consistent. All portray the same message in blogs, videos, infographics, social media posts, *etc*. You can write blogs and social media posts and submit articles to relevant publications if this appeals to you. You could do a guest blog post on someone else's blog too. You can do this before launching your business to build up your online presence and show expertise when you launch. There is some back history for people to look through too, or if people search online for you, you have a well-developed and various online professional presence.

Keep adding to this throughout your business life, then constantly re-assess and re-evaluate it to ensure the message is consistent. With multiple channels, people can reach out and engage with you on whatever medium works best for them at a convenient time. People need to encounter your business seven times before they may become a customer, so the more channels you're on, make this engagement happen more swiftly.

Google looks at your assets across the web, and how consistent they are when it ranks you, so this is a crucial reason to be consistent, to rank more highly. When you have an online asset and identity, it performs better with others than it would on its own. Make sure the information you provide is identical across sites. This includes every detail of your business address, *etc*. This is because Google will look for consistency of knowledge when it determines your credibility and ranking. So, do check every detail. Regardless of Google, customers would lose their trust in you if they see inconsistencies online.[6]

Ensure your Website is SEO friendly

Websites can take a while to gain footfall and traction, but optimizing their search engine can speed things up to get customers. WordPress and Squarespace allow you to set up your website easily. If you don't have SEO skills yourself, it's worth investing some money to get some assistance from professionals with this. Website creation is the first step, but you may also want to evaluate it occasionally to ensure that your search terms are still working for you.

Use Social Media

Social Media will get your message out there to the public. You can do targeted advertising to specific groups if you choose to do so. It can be worth looking at what other companies similar to you and at a similarly early stage do regarding advertising *(don't put too much money into advertising at this stage).*[7]

Social media can be time-consuming; one method can be to have a blog post and quote experts, who may share the content too. Using *'Facebook Groups'* can be a helpful way to find clients – *search for groups relevant to Business Consulting.*[8] You could consider answering questions as an expert on community groups such as Reddit or Slack groups. It's worth building your online reputation when you start your business and run it throughout your time because it lends you legitimacy and allows you to build relationships with customers.

Update your LinkedIn profile – this is a critical place where people search for people with the skills they need. It will help if you get your LinkedIn connections to over 500+ people and have some recommendations. Put your company name and the title of whatever Business Consulting service you offer – and a bit of a description about your services offered. This is good to be ready for when you open your business so that, again, you have this online presence, and people can search for you and add you as a connection.[9]

Be prepared to speak at events or online

Even as a start-up, speaking at events can raise awareness of your business. The right time to do this will depend on your level of expertise. If you have an area of expertise, different hubs or Chambers of Commerce are often keen to find speakers, and this allows you to share your knowledge, sets you up as an expert who people will think of or refer to when they need help, and you can network.[10] You could also be a guest on a podcast or YouTube channel, which can produce new clients. If you're asking to be on someone's podcast or YouTube channel, this shouldn't be just about self-promotion but also add some value to their show.[11]

Look at Job Boards

Depending on what area you will be consulting about, various job boards are relevant to your niche. You can do this at the start of your business, when you are trying to find new clients, or at any time when you'd like to bring more clients into your business.

Your existing contacts

Contact your family, friends, and other people in your address book. Let everyone know what you're doing and how your services could help them or people they know. You can do this with emails and social media messages too. If you haven't had contact with people for years, I won't contact them out of the blue; only contact people you know pretty well. Be open about looking for work - tell friends and family, coworkers *(if appropriate)*, current clients, past clients, anyone who knows a lot of people, any networks you belong to, etc. People are generally kind and will try to refer people your way if they can.[12]

Free work initially

This is a contentious topic, understandably, and you'll find people who sit on both sides of the fence with this. If you're offering a service, you should value it enough to deserve to receive financial compensation for it. But, if you're starting, don't have any clients, and haven't yet built up a reputation, you could offer a *'small task'* to a client for free and request that they provide you with a testimonial.

You could find these first clients by looking at universities near you; or a council, a hospital or medical center, charities, or non-profit organizations *(with missions/philosophies that mirror yours)* that seem in need of the consulting you offer. Or just large prominent employers near you, people who employ a lot of staff. You could volunteer to *SCORE* Business Mentors or Micro Mentor, which would match you to a business that wants a mentor. By doing this free work, they have nothing to lose, and there's no risk. Following the job, they will know of your services in the future should they need any other work or recommend you to others. You gain experience and a good reference which may sway other clients to ask you for help based on this experience.

Some people will want you to do this; others may be *'wary'* of free work – *this is OK and normal.* If you can find a client with a large following, their testimonial will help you gain more clients. Suppose you have created something in the past that relates to your business simply because you wanted to and were passionate about it. In that case, this is a way of showing how credible you are, *i.e.* If you created a website as a student at university for a local charity that became very active and popular and brought the charity a good amount of income/funding.

This approach shows you care about what you do. If you don't have the experience to back your credibility up, working for free will give you the experience you can prove you've got in the future. So while working for free doesn't earn you anything initially, it can be a worthwhile investment to help you make more in the future.[13] You can try this strategy out before starting your own consulting business; it's an excellent way to check that you're interested in the work and gain relevant and current experience.

Develop a thick skin

If you ask people if they want your services and say no, don't take this personally! There could be many reasons why they don't need your services currently. But, by contacting them, they're aware of you for the future, and you have no idea when they may contact you when they need your help. Always be professional, helpful, and upbeat. You need to have this approach from day one of starting your business.

Cold Contacts

One way to find clients is to go to Google and search for the type of people you think your business consulting business could assist. If you then go to p.2 and either email or phone these people to let them know how you feel you could help them. If you are offering marketing, or website design, for example, going to page two, it allows you to say something along the lines of: *"I noticed you're on page two, for XXX, and I'd like to help you to rank higher."* This can often be a helpful 'in' with business owners.[14]

This approach is also beneficial in launching your business because arranging meetings and a few discussions can take time to convert a cold contact into a client. So, if the company is mainly ready to go, and there are around 2-3 weeks until you officially launch, I would start cold contact calls *(providing you've some experience to back up what you could assist them with)*.

Consider a Coworking Space

If you're working from home, it can be more challenging to find clients. If you choose a coworking space, it's great to network and partner with others who don't offer the same service. You can learn from others about tips and tricks for running a business.

If you're in New York, Workville is a popular coworking space. In Hollywood, LA, there is NeueHouse; in Chicago and other locations, there are WeWork spaces; in Houston, there's the Work Lodge; there's Bok in Philadelphia; Downtown Works in San Diego; Common Desk in Dallas; Intelligent Office in Jacksonville; Refinery Nashville in Nashville and many others. Simply Google Coworking

Spaces for your area and look around to see which seems the best fit for you.[15]

Before launching your business, you can think about whether this would be a suitable environment for you. Or you could consider it slightly down the line if you'd like to move from home, which can feel isolated *(depending on your nature)*, to working with colleagues around you.

Ensure you're presentable

Our skills should speak louder than appearance, but people still judge a book by its cover. You should ensure you're presentable for the start of opening your business *(and possibly before for meetings with banks, refinance, or investors. while your appearance doesn't affect your ability, your professional exterior will reassure people)*.

Communicate professionally

Ensure you spell-check emails or replies to messages and your social media posts. Ensure you communicate verbally as best you can. You could decide to invest in software such as Grammarly, but don't forget that MS Word has its spelling and grammar checker. Other alternatives to Grammarly include ProWritingAid and Hemingway App, SentenceCheckup.com, and Reverso. You should strive to communicate professionally at all stages of your business, with all posts, emails, letters, and any communication anywhere, as it reflects your business.

⋆ ⋆ ⋆

Action Point:

- Write a list of the steps you will take to try to win your first clients. As a starting point, it may help you to complete the boxes below to brainstorm your ideas about who you'll contact:

1. Networking: who could you network with? Consider community groups, Eventbrite, Meetup, Lunchclub, Business Hubs, breakfast clubs, conferences)

Example: *Become a member of the Rural Enterprise Business Hub; Attend the Eventbrite seminar on the 16th of July; attend the Business Breakfast on the 20th of July; attend the Entrepreneurial conference on 10th August.*

2. Competitors: ***make a list of your competitors – could you collaborate with them?***

Example: *James Jones Business Consulting firm. Emailed and meeting arranged to discuss collaboration 1st August.*

3. Social Media: Blog post – professionals? Reddit, Slack?

Example: *Blog post with 2 professionals, in hope they will share post to their following too. Contribute to 2 discussion boards.*

```
┌─────────────────────────────────────────────┐
│                                               │
│                                               │
│                                               │
│                                               │
│                                               │
│                                               │
└─────────────────────────────────────────────┘
```

4. Website SEO

Example: Get quotes from at least 3 companies who can assist with SEO

```
┌─────────────────────────────────────────────┐
│                                               │
│                                               │
│                                               │
│                                               │
│                                               │
│                                               │
└─────────────────────────────────────────────┘
```

5. Speaking: where could you speak?

Example: Hub Event with Chamber of Commerce on 1st September. Contact host of podcast.

```
┌─────────────────────────────────────────────┐
│                                               │
│                                               │
│                                               │
│                                               │
│                                               │
│                                               │
└─────────────────────────────────────────────┘
```

6. Writing: What could you write about?

Example: List 3 topics that you could blog on – i.e., acquiring trustees for business; seeking business funding; setting up an e-commerce site.

┌─────────────────────────────────────┐
│   │
│   │
│   │
│   │
│   │
└─────────────────────────────────────┘

7. Job Boards: make a list of job boards relevant to your area of expertise

Example: Upwork, Freelancer

┌─────────────────────────────────────┐
│   │
│   │
│   │
│   │
│   │
└─────────────────────────────────────┘

8. Existing Contacts: who do you know?

Example: Family members, friends, neighbors, clubs you belong to etc.

┌─────────────────────────────────────┐
│   │
│   │
│   │
│   │
│   │
└─────────────────────────────────────┘

9. Free work? Where would it benefit you to offer some free work?

Example: The University, Local Government Council

```


```

10. LinkedIn Profile: Is it up to date?
Example: Yes

```


```

11. Cold Contacts: Who could you email or phone?
Example: Do Internet Searches for companies that look like they'd benefit from the consulting service you offer, and email or phone them. Make a list of possible ones to contact.

```


```

HOW TO PROSPECT YOUR CUSTOMERS: NETWORKING, LEVERAGING EXISTING PARTNERSHIPS

Prospecting customers is about finding them and ensuring that you have plenty of work in your pipeline for the future.[16] There are many ways to do this, including sending mail to them, handing out business cards, advertising, cold calling, etc. 94% of people looking for consultants to help their business will do their online research too. It is worth booking time into your calendar each day to do prospecting because research has shown that the top 81% of salespeople spend 4 hours or more on sales-related activities.[17]

This is an activity that, in the long run, as the business scales, could be outsourced or delegated or handed over to a team member because it falls out of the core expertise area and may take your focus away from the consulting services you offer.

Identify your dream customer

Know all about them and where to find them.

Offer different pricing structures for customers

Low-ticket and high-ticket. You can pull your dream customer into your *'circle of influence'* with a free *(or inexpensive offer)*, then build up trust and offer them the following product or service on your pricing strategy ladder.[18]

Find your dream 100

10 websites they spend time on, 15 Facebook groups they belong to, 50 influencers they follow on Facebook and Instagram, 30 podcasts they listen to, 40 email newsletters they subscribe to, 20 blogs they read, 20 YouTube channels they subscribe to. You can work by commenting on these sites or buy your way in by paying for ads.

Funnels

Offer people a free resource in return for their email – *it could be a downloadable PDF, e-Book, or a short video course.* Another technique funnel is to offer a webinar that appeals to your perfect clients. You will need to do follow-ups to convert as many people as possible.[19]

Partner with other businesses

Think about if it would be beneficial to partner with other companies so that they drive clients to you, and you bring clients to them. Someone who does web design could partner with a marketing agency that doesn't build websites, and they could both send clients to one another.

If you don't have office space but wish to meet with clients at a local coffee shop, you could partner with them so that they benefit from the drinks at meetings you hold there; in turn, they could advertise your flier or business cards for other people to take.

Follow up with previous clients

Don't ask about a sale immediately. If you had a client in the past and they aren't using your services, reach out to them and show genuine interest in how they are and how their life is going. This will jog their memory of you, and should they need your services in the future, you're freshly in their mind as a nice, friendly, and caring person.

Use Your Biggest Fans

If you have clients who love your services, ask them for a referral or encourage them to sell your services for a commission.

Consider a CRM

If you start to gain a large number of clients, a CRM will enable you to make your work smoother with workflows and allow you to communicate with customers easily. You can also share with other team members via it if your team expands, and many jobs can become automated, which speeds up repetitive tasks.

Ask customers questions

Ask questions and listen carefully to their responses. Find out their challenges/problems and how you could resolve them. What are their problems, and how can you help to solve them? What do they need help with? What is their budget to solve the problem? Do they know what services you offer? Where do they hang out online – *Facebook, LinkedIn, Reddit, etc.?* What keeps your customer awake at night? Knowing your customer better will allow you to offer what they need.

ℬ ℬ ℬ

Action Points:

- Have a go at filling out the boxes below to see how you could get new customers

1. Dream Customer: take some time to list what your dream customer would be

Example: Spends X amount of money per month; is easy to get along with and communicate with; reliable to pay invoices quickly; gives creative freedom; feel valued and appreciated by etc.

2. Pricing Structure: What will you offer and at what cost? Is there a low and high offer?

Example: Presentations cost X. Workshops cost X. Website design costs X. Review and Report Costs X.

[ ]

3. Dream 100: Facebook, websites, influencers, podcasts, email newsletters, blogs, YouTube channels – where your clients spend their time

Example: First Man photography site; Kofi sites; Photography Daily; Chris Sale; Mali Davies etc.

[ ]

4. Funnels: Could you offer a free resource? What will your follow up email say?

Example: Here is a free short booklet on X topic. Follow up email: I've noticed you've not taken up the offer of X and I didn't want you to miss out.

[ ]

5. Partner? Any businesses you could partner with?

Example: Contact X Web design to see if they're interested in us sign-posting customers to one another.

```


```

6. Previous clients? Any previous clients you could catch up with?

Example: Contact Joe Bloggs, John Smith, Jane Doe not to offer services specifically – just to ask how they are, or update them?

```


```

HOW TO KEEP CLIENTS

"Be nicer to your customers than your competitors."

— RICHARD REED, INNOCENT DRINKS

Research has shown that it can cost five times more to gain a new customer than to retain a current one.[20] Other research shows that *"repeat purchases by established customers usually require less marketing effort – as much as 90% less."*[21] Keeping customers is about providing outstanding customer service by being customer-centric and thinking backward. Any decision you take must benefit your customer, and you must conveniently meet their needs with excellent communication and customer relation skills. Having an *'interdepen-*

dent relationship' with your clients can be important where you have high levels of mutual trust and interaction. Always be prepared with contingency plans that can make for a successful relationship.[22]

Here are some valuable tips for retaining your customers:

"If you are working on a product that's going to be consumer-facing, then feedback is invaluable. You should be out there being brave and talking to people and asking for feedback as much as possible."

– Emily Brooke, Co-founder of Blaze.

1. Keep in Contact Regularly

Update customers, ask for feedback, and check their levels of customer satisfaction; if you don't get 10 out of 10, enquire what it would take to make it a 10; if you gain 10, enquire about what they especially appreciate.[23] Check expectations at the start, keep them in the loop throughout the project, and give weekly update reports if it's a long project.[24] As part of this, avoid *'pitch teams'* who get customers eager about a project, only for the customer to find that once signed up, they're working with different people they have never met. People will initially form a connection with those they meet, like them, and want them to see the project through. It feels like a betrayal if they're just passed on to another team member to deal with. When you stay connected with customers, use the best communication methods for them.[25]

2. Create Valuable Authoritative Content

If you have new insights or new opportunities, your customers will feel you're the most up-to-date source of knowledge on it. They will share your content or recommend you to others, and you can share this via blogs, guest posts, LinkedIn articles, social media posts, short videos, and infographics. Always remember to keep your content consistent across all channels.

3. The Importance of Follow-up - Be Quick to Respond to Enquiries

Ideally, you should answer emails within 24 hours or quicker. This is to get your clients the best results and the most sales. When you follow up with clients, what you're doing is building a relationship with them.[26]

Even if you send a brief 'holding' email letting people know you've received their query and will respond asap, this will help you. Immediate contact with customers after their questions will prevent them from becoming angry or frustrated at a lack of response. It will also save you dealing with double the number of emails if the customer emails you again to check because they haven't had a response to the first. If someone has called you and left a message, be sure to return their phone call quickly. Because many people either don't return calls or are slow to reply to emails, a fast response may place you at a good advantage.[27]

Make yourself accessible to meet customer needs when they need your assistance. You should also follow up if you've cold-called someone again to build on the relationship to stay fresh in their mind. If you send follow-up emails to customers and ensure they are relevant to the interests and needs of the client, it's good to include a call to action within your emails and a link to your webpage. It can be a good idea to keep a database of your customer contact information *(update it after every customer contact)* and keep any business cards you receive. You could send weekly blog updates via email and newsletters. Research has shown that companies who get back to customers within an hour of a query are seven times more likely to gain that person as a customer.[28]

4. Be Confident and Well Informed

Clients want you to be the expert, so act decisively and confidently. It is critical in business, especially in consulting, to be well informed and keep up with the trends of the market; the market is unpredictable and can change quickly. Entrepreneurs need to try to stay ahead of the curve. Ways to do this include staying connected with customers where they naturally want to be, not where you want them to be. Keep up to date with technology.

Have a multi-channel approach because they may show different nuances; always be prepared to change and don't assume it will continue because something worked in the past.[29]

If you think you're likely to be asked specific questions by prospective or current clients, be well prepared and do your research. Ensure, though, that you communicate clearly to customers without the need for jargon. Ensure that any data/statistics you present are relevant to their business/industry.

Take time to self-educate, be self-motivated, and inspire yourself daily. Read books, attend courses and conferences, watch videos and documentaries, and read articles or blogs that you can learn from that give you the skills to do something better. Keep moving towards your goals and improving yourself daily; this will help you succeed.[30]

5. Listen Carefully

Listen to your customers carefully and value that they're experts in their business. You must take their ideas and input on board because they know their customers better than you. Try your hardest to understand what they do in their business so you can realize their goals, aims, brand, and market.[31]

Try to connect at a personal level, too; if your client says they're tired because they had a busy children's party at the weekend, remember that, and in the subsequent call, ask if they've managed to get some rest since the party. These little communication cues don't take long and can go a long way to building a better relationship. Remember that every customer is individual and unique and wants your services tailored specifically to their needs.

Look at what customers say on blogs, videos, and TikTok, look at their comments and hear their views, ask existing customers, ask customers who aren't interested in your consulting services why they're not buying, observe and ask questions.[32]

6. Personal Touches

Anything you can do to show your customers that you care about them will help. So, perhaps sending a hand-written Christmas card shows that you value them.

Another suggestion is that you could send them a small gift or provide a business lead for them that helps them get more business. Another personal touch that people appreciate is hand-written thank-you notes; this is why Peter Drucker believes he was successful because he sent out 12 thank-you cards daily.[33]

You could occasionally give a *'no charge'* invoice, which will help the customers to remember you. You can also offer promotions and discounts to good customers to show that you appreciate their loyalty to your business.[34] Always be kind and empathic.

7. Under promise and over deliver

If you do this the other way round and don't meet what you've promised, customers will feel disappointed! Unhappy customers will typically let 20 people know they're down, damaging your business, whereas a happy customer generally tells 3-4 people.[35]

It's far better to under-promise and exceed this. Try to ensure that you do jobs by the date and time you've said you would do them too because, again, customers will know they can depend upon you.[36] If you can make your client's business successful, you will also thrive as a consulting business.[37]

8. Be proactive

It's good to constantly think about how you can improve your customer's business; get more value for money; be more productive by doing this; it shows that you truly invest yourself in helping their business improve. You could also use their services and products; this is a great way to build loyalty.

9. Manage expectations and seek clarity

Be clear about what you will and won't do for customers, so there is no confusion. At the beginning of a working relationship, be clear about their expectations and how you will meet them. Always aim for clarity. If you ever make a mistake, be open about it, and tell the customer exactly what you will do to fix it. By fixing mistakes, 70% of unhappy customers will remain loyal, providing the error has been appropriately dealt with.

10. Convenience for Customers, not You

Make it easy for your customers to contact and do business with you. Things need to be convenient for them and not you, and you need to eliminate any barriers or hassles for the customer.

An example of this would be if you are working with international clients, ensure that you meet with them at a time convenient to their time zone *(even if this means it is not typical working hours for you)*.

Another example is if your personal preference is to communicate by email. Still, if you know that your customer likes a more in-person approach, you could make an effort to meet in person, or at least speak over the phone or via Zoom, so it's more face-to-face than an email where you cannot hear the tone of voice. It would be best if you aimed to be a resource for your customers and try your best to help them.[38]

11. Treat Employees Well

If your business grows and scales up and you need to hire employees with time, ensure that you treat them well. Firstly, it's the right thing to do, but if you don't, understandably, they may not represent your company well to customers.

12. Form an Advisory Panel

This is to get to know your client's needs and adapt your business around these to ensure you are client-oriented.

Action Points:

Checklist

1. Do you ask your clients for feedback?
2. Do you keep up to date with developments in your field and could you share content on this?
3. Do you respond to emails/calls quickly?
4. Are you confident in your expertise?
5. Do you listen carefully about client's work and home issues?
6. Do you do personal touches? Handwritten cards?
7. Do you under-promise and over-deliver?
8. Are you proactive?
9. Are you clear and manage expectations?
10. Do you make things convenient for clients?
11. Do you treat employees well?
12. Could you form an advisory panel?

HOW TO DEVELOP/ HOW TO GET MORE OUT OF EXISTING CLIENTS

1. Ask for referrals

If you have a good relationship with your current clients, you can ask them if they would be happy to refer any other businesses to your services. When another company refers people to you, it lends a lot of weight because it's an excellent strong recommendation of how your services have helped them and how they think you could help another business.[39]

2. Cross-selling and Up-selling

Cross-selling is where you would integrate the service with other services that are connected/complement the original service. When you cross-sell, you will capture a larger market share by meeting each customer's needs. Amazon uses cross-selling when you purchase a book; they will often tell you what other related books are available and what other items were bought by other customers who purchased the book.

Up-selling is where you offer the client better services. In this scenario, you may either offer the customer more of the service you provided or more of something else. So a more expensive version of what they already purchased.[40] You could create packages with optional add-ons, like special deals, promotions, or bundling.

An example could be providing a copy for a website and offering SEO services or a weekly blog. You need to highlight all the cost savings, security, peace of mind, or the fact you have an *'all-in-one'* solution for your client and do this with stats of ROI if possible. It's important too to pick the right moment to upsell with your client, some people at year-end need to use their budgets or could be just about to give a brand-new budget, so this is always a valuable time.[41]

3. Give thought to a customer's long-term or lifetime value (LTV)

In doing this, you could contemplate how recently they've used your services and, on average, how much monetary value they bring you. While this all sounds a bit calculating, it makes good business sense to invest more time in customers who use you frequently and spend more. If it comes to a point where you need to free up more time to spend on high-value customers, then you may decide to *'cull'* work for less desirable customers.[42]

۞   ۞   ۞

Action Points:

- Have a go at filling out the boxes below to give help you understand how you can get more from current customers:

1. Referrals: Think about who you could ask for a referral. Who was pleased with previous work you've done?

Example: Joe Bloggs from the Government Department seemed exceptionally pleased with the website I designed.

2. Cross-selling and Up-selling: Can you integrate the service with any others that are connected/compliment it? Could you move your client onto more or better services?

Example: A customer who pays for services on retainer – could agree to take a 40-hour retainer, rather than just 20 hours as previously.

3. Customers Long-Term or Life-Time Value: Give thought to who your most valuable customers are – so that if a time comes to prioritize services you can do this with best effect.

Example: Customer X spends X amount reliably, consistently per month, they're easy to work with, and likely to need continuing assistance.

CONCRETE PRO TIP FROM EXPERTS

1. **Jeff Bezos**'s key tip is to *"listen to your customers. They should always be the most important person in the room."* Bezos' mission was for Amazon to become the Earth's most customer-centric company; it was a high aim. That's why this book chapter is *'Client's First'* because they must always be your focus! Bezos invested a lot of time in going out to listen to customers and constantly researching. As I'm sure you know, Amazon initially started selling books, videos, and music. Bezos picked 1,000 customers and asked them, besides these things, *"what would you like to see us sell?"* He listened to them and followed this through, filling their needs.[43]

2. **Jack Ma**, who founded the Alibaba Group, is equally customer focused as Jeff Bezos, this is something they have in common, and clearly, it has been the secret of their enormous success. Ma's key phrase is *"forget about your competitors; just focus on your customers."* Ma also has a loyalty program model where customers can be co-creators, with gaming elements and time-sensitive mobile promotions. Another critical expression from his autobiography Alibaba: The House That Jack Ma Built is *"Customers first, employees second, and shareholders third."*[44]

3. **Bill Gates** suggests, *"your most unhappy customers are your greatest source of learning"*[45], This recaps the earlier point in the section about *'how to keep clients'* staying connected regularly and asking for feedback to gauge their satisfaction levels. Gates suggests that if a customer isn't 100% happy, then you need to learn how to improve

their customer experience, and when you do so, this will build their loyalty to you because they can see that you've done something about it, you care and want them to be happy.

4.The Big Four are the world's largest consulting firms, which account for nearly 40% of the consulting industry; these include PwC, Deloitte, EY, and KPMG. PwCs text on its website shows how important clients are to them *"Our clients come to PwC for innovative and imaginative solutions to help them meet the challenges they face and capitalize on the opportunities."*[46]
Similarly, Deloitte has a section called *"Clients first – providing what they need."*[47] EY's statement directly addresses the client and says how their company will help *"realize your ambition and support you to expand, transform, integrate, govern and finance your business."*[48] KPMG is similar to PwC in that they show the benefit they offer to their clients: *"Helping our clients thrive. KPMG professionals are delivering solutions for our client's biggest challenges."*[49]

The next chapter will focus on writing a proposal that aims to give you the best chances for success; learning how to pitch the proposal; setting up a pricing structure of fees for your services; implementing a sales plan and cycle, along with the usual pro tips of do's and don'ts from experts.

KEY TAKEAWAYS FROM THIS CHAPTER

1. To win clients, you can: network; collaborate with competitors; use social media; have your website search engine optimized; speak at events; write blogs; look at job boards; contact everyone you know; consider working for free to build up experience and testimonials; don't take rejections personally; update LinkedIn; let people know you're looking for work; approach cold contacts; consider a co-working space; be presentable and communicate professionally.

2. To prospect customers, which will help you to find a pipeline of

future work you can: put the time in your day to do this; identify your dream customer; offer different pricing structures; know what social media, email newsletters, and YouTube channels your customers spend time on; funnel customers with a free resource and follow-up; partner with other businesses; follow up with previous clients; use your biggest fans for referrals or to sell at a commission; consider a CRM and question customers and listen to them.

3. To keep/retain your customers, you can: have regular contact with them; ask for feedback; create valuable content; respond quickly to inquiries; be confident about expertise; listen carefully to customers about work and non-work issues; do personal touches such as hand-written cards; under-promise and over-deliver; be proactive; be clear and manage expectations; be convenient for your clients; treat employees well, so they present your company well; and form an advisory panel.

4. To develop and get more out of existing clients, you could ask for referrals, cross-sell and up-sell and consider customers' long-term or lifetime value (LTV).

6

IMPLEMENTATION

This sixth step to starting and growing your own consulting business from zero is all about implementation. In this chapter, I will teach how to write a proposal and how to pitch it. You will learn how to price your services with a pricing structure and plan and how to create a sales plan. There will also be, as usual, pro tips from experts, and the do's and don'ts to make your business a success.

By the end of this chapter, you will know how to:

1. Write a proposal that has a high chance of success.
2. Pitch a proposal.
3. Set up a pricing structure or plan with your fees for services.
4. Compile a sales plan and sales cycle.
5. Follow the do's and don'ts advice from experts.

HOW TO WRITE A PROPOSAL THAT HAS A HIGH CHANCE OF SUCCESS

"After all, winning business is what writing proposals are all about. Although a great proposal by itself seldom wins a deal, a bad proposal will lose one."

— *TOM SANT*

According to Tom Sant, a proposal is not a price quote because if all you give is the price, it states that all services of this type are the same, without anything unique. It's also not meant to be a bill of materials, a project plan, or a scope of work. It should not be about your company history. A proposal should be a sales document that leads to an agreement to work together. The proposal's purpose is to move the sales process towards closure.

A consulting proposal is a document that will win you the client. It will let the client know what steps you will take to sort out the problems they are struggling with. It must have your ideas, strategies, and set the terms and conditions to do the job. It's an agreement between you and your client that sets expectations on both sides before you start the job.

Without wanting to *'blow my own trumpet,'* I think writing proposals is one of my particular strengths. The ones I write are usually successful, and I have no issue gaining jobs and customers. Through this chapter, I'll assist you in writing winning proposals with a high chance of success.

I tend to write the proposals once I've met with the client and had a good discussion. I always ensure that I understand their issues and desires, check details, show them what they will gain from the process, highlight my value proposition, ask for feedback, and then put forward a proposal.

An **excellent** consulting proposal should include:

1. A cover page
2. An executive summary kept to one page *(concise overview of goals/requirement)*
3. A project outline/scope of work
4. Deliverables
5. Project fees & timeline
6. A proposal summary[1]

It's a good idea to create a consulting proposal template that you feel happy with *(there are lots of templates you can find online)*.

Alternatively, you can check:

www.theconsultingclub.com/free-resources

where I've added my personal favorite template. You can download it for free and adjust it to your needs.

The content

If we dive deep into the content of a proposal, always remember to stress the benefits to the client, *i.e.*, *"I can save you 20 hours a month in lost productivity"*, *"I can increase your profits by 20%"*, or *"I can drive 25% more visitors to your website"*. It will help the client to picture himself better and envision the benefits of your service. If you don't emphasize this, they may go for a cheaper scenario because they don't realize the experience or quality of service they'll get with you. It is critical to market and showcase why your knowledge, qualification, and skills make you the best consultant to help them.

Another thing I like to do is to mention other solutions that I offer *(see the upselling section of the previous chapter)*.

For example, if you were offering bookkeeping, you could also mention your tax-preparation services; this bundled *'whole'* solution may set you apart from others who submit a proposal. Or they may want these services at a later stage.

If what you offer is technical, ensure you don't use jargon and that you explain things clearly for a non-technical audience. If they're seeking your experience, they are most likely not experts in this area.

Pre-work is critical

To successfully turn a potential client into a new client, you need to take some initial steps before you present them with your consulting proposal:

1. Phone or meet with the client via Zoom/Teams, *etc.* This approach will build trust.[2]
2. Ask the questions that show your client's business needs and how you'll meet them. Statistics have shown that asking 11-14 questions when meeting prospective clients can give a 74% success rate. Find out what challenges they are facing, what they need a solution for, what results from what they're hoping for and by when *etc.* Ask open-ended questions to get more out of them, and listen to what they say.[3] Ensure you understand their needs.
3. Show the client how you will meet their needs with things they can measure. *E.g.*, you will improve sales by 20%. You will enhance website footfall by 15% *etc.*
4. Agree on expectations for when you will provide the deliverables.[4]
5. Create a professional consulting proposal and get the client to sign this before starting work.

※ ※ ※

Action Points:

Checklist

Before your Consulting Proposal

1. Have you asked your prospective client questions?
2. Have you told your client about the other services you could offer them?
3. Have you shown clients the benefits/gains from your services?

For your Consulting Proposal

1. You can download a free-template that I have created for you.
2. You can easily download it by scanning the QR code at the beginning of the book and/or visit the website of the consulting club here: https://theconsultingclub.com/ or simply send me an email to: matthew@ theconsultingclub.com
3. Have you checked spelling/grammar in a proposal?
4. Have you avoided jargon/technical language?

HOW TO PITCH A PROPOSAL (SALES PITCH IN CONSULTING)

"Approach each customer with the idea of helping him or her solve a problem or achieve a goal, not of selling a product or service."

— BRIAN TRACY

After you have created your consulting proposal, you need to sell it; this applies to clients, bankers, and investors. Sales skills don't always come naturally to people, but, as you might know, without selling your services, you won't get new clients.[5]

. . .

Selling a proposal comes with pitching it. Try to *"deliver an experience, not a speech"*.[6] Be as immersive as you can for the client, tell them relatable stories, and if there's anything practical you can show people or let people take away, do it because it will make the experience more memorable.

You need to be confident about what you're selling; for example, QVC, a shopping channel, doesn't say that they sell items; they say that *"they sell things to make you more beautiful, intelligent, or wealthy"*. Steve Jobs doesn't sell computers but a *"bicycle for our mind."* Create your OWN story and make sure that you can explain it in a few words - think of it like your own slogan.

The elevator pitch

An elevator pitch is an offer that comes across as meaningful and authentic; it should not feel like a forced sales pitch. It must be brief, concise, and as creative as possible. They need to remember you.

It's maybe your unique chance to make a real connection, and you need to have it ready and be adaptable for any given opportunity. I recommend it to be as short as possible *(around 30 seconds)* while covering the most critical points.

Why 30 seconds? Well, people have short attention spans so you better practice your pitch, because in this short amount of time you should include:

- Introducing yourself
- Presenting the problem
- Offering your solution
- Sharing your value proposition
- Stating a call to action

Tips on how to pitch

Be natural, make eye contact, be appropriate to your audience, and use real-world examples.[7] Your value proposition gives the audience an answer to why they should choose your solution over competitors. Be genuine and show passion for it.[8]

How to get ready

Start by capturing all the ideas you want to put across, then think about the best medium to communicate them.

Things I have used in the past that usually work well in complementing my pitch are some kind of visual support such as demonstrations, PowerPoints, or videos. If you're using PowerPoint, keep the slides simple and uncluttered. Ideally, just one picture and one line of text per slide. Research has proven that people remember 10% of the information they receive, which increases to 65% if you add pictures. Avoid using jargon; if technical terms are necessary, ensure you explain these in simple terms. Rehearse your material until you are confident and know your timings. Use stories, metaphors, analogies, and props wherever you can.[9]

What you should address

Often in pitches, people talk about their qualifications, which makes sense to a certain extent. Still, you must show how your capabilities will solve problems and address your client's needs to make them relevant.[10] When you pitch, it shouldn't be about you and your company but how you'll meet the client's needs. It's about them!

This is one of the biggest mistakes I made early in my career, which turned out to be a huge learning experience. In the beginning, I got a lot of 'closed doors' because I was focusing my efforts on selling my expertise and company rather than selling how I was going to address their issue. I even noticed that people turned off their attention once I started mentioning things such as how I started my own consulting business. They did not care. They genuinely only cared about how I was going to solve THEIR problem. From this, I learned to always provide a straightforward solution to my client's issues without all the fluff. This is one of the reasons why this book is focused on finding solutions for **you**, and it's not about my story.

You need to show you have listened to your client, re-cap their issues, and see if anything has changed since you last spoke. Then address each of their problems and show how you've helped clients with a similar challenge, your approach, and the result. Propose a solution, and ask their thoughts on that. Then keep addressing their other issues one by one.[11]

It's better to present *'benefits'* rather than *'features'*, always showing how what you're offering could benefit your client. By *'benefits'*, you can talk about your solution's impact on the customer's business and mention Return on Investment (ROI) to them. Having precise figures of how much they'll spend but how much they stand to gain will give the client clarity on how they decide to spend their budget.[12]

Because of technology like Zoom, Skype, Teams, etc., you can pitch your proposals far more easily across the world, without having to get to a location to meet people in person physically.[13] Thanks to this, your potential clients can be anywhere in the world; you should not limit yourself to your local community.

Use the right words and approach

When you pitch a proposal, rather than suggesting *'if'* the customer decides to use you, talk more about *'how'* your company will provide them with different cost scenarios according to which services they require. You can give a baseline cost, then various *'add-ons'* dependent on other services they may wish to take advantage of.[14] Something that has helped me a lot throughout my career was to adopt a proven sales strategy to connect with customers called *The Challenger Sale model (based on a book by Matthew Dixon and Brent Adamson)*[15], which focuses on understanding the customer's business.

Challengers love to debate, pushing customers to get out of their comfort zone. This method is less about building relationships and instead more about teaching clients how to solve their problems. It's how you, as a consultant, can take control of any conversation. The most critical steps of this sale methodology include:

1. **The warm-up** — You need to build credibility with clients and show that you understand the issues the client has. You must have researched thoroughly before meeting with them to know their pain points. You want the client to agree that this is a problem.

2. **Re-frame** — Instead of posing the clients' issues as problems, you need to 're-frame' them as a growth opportunity. At this point, you need to convince the client that their ideas to solve the problem won't work. As part of this stage, you could list the typical costs associated with solving the issue, making the client worry about these.

Then you can announce that you have more effective *(and possibly cheaper or more cost-effective)* methods. You have taken control of the process by challenging them and getting them to consider that the solution they thought was best may not be the case.
You must be fearless and confident that your alternative solutions are the best. You are trying to get the customer to think differently rather than gain a sale at this stage.

3. **Emotions are relatable** — If a customer can relate by identifying with other customer stories who have had similar issues, then hear about the benefit they received; they will be able to connect to this story and imagine the benefits for them too. If you can use visuals when you tell the story, this will keep in the customer's mind more than just words.

4. **The value proposition** — Keep focused on solutions. Show that you can solve the client's issues. Show a positive future should they act. If the customer needs any explanation, take the time to go through this with the client.

5. **Show that your Consultancy is the answer** — Using steps 1-4, you

have led the conversation from the beginning, and here you're just reiterating that you have the perfect solution to their issues.[16]

When you need to cold call...

A good sales script can be essential if you're cold-calling customers by phone. Peter Strohkorb writes that in general

"cold calling gives sales reps a bad reputation and ruins prospecting for the entire sales industry."

He continues to say that *"the only time that cold calling has half a chance of working is if you have something significant up your sleeve that is of vital importance to them and their business."* If you have something like that, then [look at] the section below about Challenger/ Disruptive/ and Provocative Selling.[17]

Some steps to achieve this include:

1. Immediately hooking them with why they should care about the service you offer and add the business impact that this will offer.
2. Giving your pitch ideally in just one sentence *(see the information about elevator pitches above)*.
3. Asking the customer if you can give them any more information.
4. Asking the customer questions about their specific needs to see if the customer is a good match for your business.
5. Finding out more about when they'll decide if they're interested in using your services and whether there are budget constraints.
6. Ensuring you have meetings set up for the future with them.

※ ※ ※

Action Point:

- Have a go at using the Challenger Sales Model in your pitch and fill the boxes below:

1. What issue does your client have?
Example: Your client doesn't have much of an online presence.

```
┌─────────────────────────────────────────────────────────┐
│                                                           │
│                                                           │
│                                                           │
│                                                           │
│                                                           │
└─────────────────────────────────────────────────────────┘
```

2. What methods 'might' your client use to try to solve their issue? Present these and suggest why they won't work. Challenge your client's views and get them to think in a different way. *(This is the most important step).*

Example: Your client thought about creating Facebook accounts, getting a website set up, and some other social media. Explain that it's not as beneficial to have all different accounts set up, but to have them linked online, all consistent and same message.

```
┌─────────────────────────────────────────────────────────┐
│                                                           │
│                                                           │
│                                                           │
│                                                           │
│                                                           │
└─────────────────────────────────────────────────────────┘
```

3. Show how previous customers have had the same issue – and benefited from help.

Example: Company X didn't have an online presence either. They tried to set up their own website. It was perhaps more damaging because it looked unprofessional. Until you designed a good website for them and linked their Social Media accounts. Consistency – meet Google algorithms etc.

---

4. Show how their issue can be solved. The future is positive.

Example: It's entirely possible to set up an online presence, with a website, social media, blog – all linked and it will drive sales to the business (and make it easier for customer to buy).

---

5. Show how you're the best person to assist them with this.

Example: I've done this for companies X, Y and Z, and on average, their sales have increased by 12%.

> *"If you've got the power to raise prices without losing business to a competitor, you've got a perfect business. And if you have to have a prayer session before raising the price by 10 percent, then you've got a terrible business."*
>
> — WARREN BUFFETT

When first growing your business, it can be challenging to determine what price you will charge for your services. Price is a perception of value, so this is up to you to choose.

When trying to estimate your value, try to address the following questions:

1. How will you increase your client's long-term financial gain when you offer your services?

2. How will you get rid of any obstacles they have?

3. How will you give insights that will make their business more successful?

4. How will you create more online traffic for them?

5. What will be the results of your help?

6. Think about your expertise and your skill-set – how much experience do you have? *(the more you have, the more you can charge)*

7. Is it more cost-efficient for you to do the work than them?

8. Will you offer strategy consulting *(business growth strategies/beating the competition)* or management consulting *(specific business strategies in HR, finance, or IT)*?[18]

9. Does your client have the time to do the work?

10. Consider your location – *depending on where you live, it may mean you can charge higher consulting fees.*

11. Try to estimate how long it will take you to do the task the

client needs help with. You can consider where you want your services to fit within the market and whether you will be lower than your competitors or seen as a higher quality *(and therefore expensive)* service.[19]

12. You need to know that people will buy the product at the price you are offering, and you could conduct some market research via questionnaires/surveys to assess this. You could also look at prices online for businesses similar to yours.

13. You will need to consider in your pricing structure that you're covering all the costs associated with your service; you need to ensure that you're getting in more money than these costs to make a profit.

14. You may need to consider if there are any legal or regulatory constraints placed on how much you can charge for your services.

15. You need to have a pricing strategy that allows you to cover costs and continue to grow your business. You need to ensure that you can make a living from the price you charge. You must strike a balance that covers your costs but is not higher than what clients consider fair. Would this start a price war with your competitors if you price low?[20]

Setting your price

When you set your costs, don't put them too low because rather than being grateful for your great value, clients may think your work is low-quality if the price is too low. Similarly, if your prices are too high, some clients may not be able to afford this and may go for a more affordable alternative. Look into your industry's consulting rates, as these will vary according to industry.

You need to consider how much you are willing to work for, every person has their minimum, and they won't go below that. Over time, ensure that your price goes up to reflect your experience and success. You can also base your pricing on the customer's value. Get the customer to think about if they don't have your help to fix the issues, what consequences and business impact would occur to their business, and what might the cost be if they neglect to do something about it.[21]

Hourly/Project/Value-Based Pay?

You may wonder whether you should bill customers hourly, project, or value-based pay. When starting and growing your consulting business, I recommend billing per project rather than hourly payment because that can make you seem more of a commodity. It can also be beneficial to offer clients three price ranges. Sometimes these are classed as bronze *(lower cost)*, silver *(medium cost)*, and gold service *(high cost)*. In this way, you allow the customer to choose their most suitable option.[22]

- **Hourly Pay**

While I wouldn't recommend hourly pay, it's worth having an hourly figure in mind so that when you have a project, and you predict how long that project will take you in hours, you have a figure in mind for how much this will cost.[23]

Hourly pay may be OK for beginners working on their first consulting projects, but once you have the expertise, it's not advisable to use an hourly method. To work out an hourly rate, you need to decide on what annual salary you want to have and divide it by 52 *(working weeks in a year)* and 40 *(hours to work each week)*. Next, increase that number by either 25% or 50%. Generally, 40% is an excellent figure to increase this by.

For example, an annual salary of $60,000 per year, divided by 52 is $1,154; divided by 40 is $28.85, plus 40% would give you an hourly rate of around $40. You are adding the 40% increase because this will go towards business expenses, overheads, taxes, etc.

Things in a business will always cost more than you initially anticipate.[24] So, take some time to work out figures that suit you. It could be that you want to work fewer weeks in a year or fewer hours in a week, so again, consider this with your figures. Every time you complete a project, increase your hourly rate by $25. You will get to a point whereby charging by the hour is no longer best for you or your clients.[25]

Having an approximate 'hourly' figure in mind will help you judge how much projects should cost based on how long you anticipate the project will take. Fixed fees are suitable for customers, as they know the price upfront, but be sure that you don't end up working much longer hours than you thought the project would take to fulfill the contract.

- **Project Based**

When you charge by the project, this relieves any concern clients have about how much the project will cost once completed, and this may help more clients to move forward because they know the costs from the outset. To set a project fee:

1. Start by writing a list of all the deliverables you will produce.
2. Work out how long each of the deliverables will take.
3. Add up the hours, and multiply this by your hourly fee, times the total by 1.5 because projects take longer than you anticipate.

So, if you worked out the deliverables would take 30 hours, your hourly fee is $100, which equals $3000. Multiplying it by 1.5 equals $4,500 for the project, ensuring this is a figure you feel happy with, to ensure that you do the best work.[26]

- **Value-Based**

Over time once you have 2-5+ years of experience, you could use value-based pricing, which is more about the results and outcomes you'll create for your client. You can use an ROI formula with them that considers *intangible + tangible + annual = value-based price.*[27]

❦ ❦ ❦

Action Points:

Checklist

1. Have you checked how much competitors charge?
2. Where do you want to fit in the market?
3. Have you done market research – *questionnaires*?
4. What do you need to cover costs & make a living?
5. Have you worked out an approximate hourly charge?

YOUR SALES PLAN AND SALES CYCLE

"Great salespeople are relationship builders who provide value and help their customers win."

— JEFFERY GITOMER

It's essential to have a very clear sales plan, and sales cycle as this will support you through selling your consulting business services, from finding a prospect to initial discussions, a proposal pitch, and delivering the services and being paid for that.[28] You will need to spend as much time getting new business as possible to the time spent providing the service.

In your sales plan, set out:

1. Where you'll find new clients – How you'll make people aware of your consulting business. What you will do after first having contact with a prospective customer *(set up a call or face-to-face meeting to discuss your offer, put in a firm proposal, and, once accepted, arrange a time to deliver the service).* You can use tools like *'Calendly'* and Acuity scheduling[29] to help clients to make appointments with you. You can add it to websites or emails; this can be a quicker way to get a meeting, rather than lots of back-and-forth messages.

2. Regularly assess your sales plan, keep metrics on how many meetings or calls it takes to close a deal and look at ways to reduce these.

3. Have targets and goals that you want to achieve. A good starting point for this can be to consider your monthly target revenue, then work backward and think about how many clients using your services you would need to achieve this.[30]

4. Think carefully about who you are targeting your service to and ensure you are trying to contact the best leads that fit this.

5. Ensure that you decline work that doesn't fit with what you want to be doing. Try to be helpful and refer potential customers to other people if possible.

6. Think long-term and build relationships for future sales. Not immediately selling to contacts allows a connection to build up. You should network as much as possible because even if people don't want to use your services now, they may do in the future.[31]

🐚 🐚 🐚

Action Point:

- Have a go at filling the boxes below:

1. New clients? Where will you find them, and make them aware? Find the decision maker at the business.
Example: word of mouth, referrals, jobs boards, adverts, cold contact

```
┌──────────────────────────────────────────────┐
│                                                │
│                                                │
│                                                │
│                                                │
│                                                │
│                                                │
└──────────────────────────────────────────────┘
```

2. What's your process once you have contact with a customer?
Example: *phone-call, Zoom meeting or face-to-face meeting.*

```
┌──────────────────────────────────────────────┐
│                                                │
│                                                │
│                                                │
│                                                │
│                                                │
│                                                │
└──────────────────────────────────────────────┘
```

3. Do you keep metrics? Can you improve these?
Example: *It typically takes 1 zoom meeting, and 3 emails to close a deal. I 'may' be able to reduce emails by being more thorough/precise with information in the first 2.*

```
┌──────────────────────────────────────────────┐
│                                                │
│                                                │
│                                                │
│                                                │
│                                                │
└──────────────────────────────────────────────┘
```

4. What sales targets/goals do you have?
Example: *In order to earn XX per month, I would need to typically take on 4 clients per month.*

[ ]

5. Who is your target audience/ideal customers? Are your leads meeting these?

Example: Target audience is XX, I can find these clients at the following places.

[ ]

6. Keep a list of the work you don't want to take or have not enjoyed to ensure you don't take any more of this in future.

Example: I didn't enjoy X job doing Y and Z, I'll not take on any further customers in that area. But to provide a good service, I could refer them to Joe Bloggs or John Smith they will appreciate how helpful I've been and in future they may need our services or recommend us to others.

[ ]

CONCRETE PRO TIPS FROM EXPERTS

1. Jeff Bezos, doesn't like people using PowerPoint presentations in their proposal pitches; he sent a memo to his senior team saying, *"No PowerPoint presentation from now on."* They can be a bit dry, too full, and repetitive, many people read from the screen, and usually, the audience could just read that for themselves. There are more engaging methods *(stories/props/analogies/narrative documents etc.)*[32]

2. Steve Jobs was excellent at pitching proposals. He employed eight techniques in his pitches:

1. Spiking curiosity in the first few seconds.
2. Building credibility by referring to previous successes.
3. Using humor and wit to earn trust.
4. Draw on competitors' pros and knock them down with solid counter-arguments.
5. Use power words and buzz words *(but not jargon)*. The word *'cutting edge'* is a good phrase.
6. Focus on the benefits.
7. Know your audience.
8. Be appreciative of their time and humble.[33]

3. Mark Zuckerberg's approach was to use money from other parts of the business to allow them to make different prices lower. I want to report his quote here as this truly inspired the way I developed my business:

"I'm pretty inclined to take whatever gains we could get from things like an app store, and just that to make the price lower our inclination is probably going to be to try to offer these products at as low of a cost as possible to be able to get them out to everyone. So, unlike other companies in this space that charge premium prices as their business model, one of our core principles is that we want to serve everything. I'm very focused on how you

create a good VR and AR device and make it, so it's $300 instead of $1000. I think that's a pretty big deal."[34]

The next chapter will focus on creating credibility and marketing your value. This approach will teach you how to sell the business to make it more credible and win notoriety. You will learn all the secrets of marketing, including the **4Ps**, place and promotion, branding, creating an online presence, positioning and marketing your value, marketing consulting services, and as always, pro tips from experts with dos and don'ts.

KEY TAKEAWAYS FROM THIS CHAPTER

1. Use your proposal to move the sales process towards closure.

2. Ensure you ask your clients lots of questions before the proposal, ideally 11 – 14, to make it 74% likely that you'll be successful in gaining work from them.

3. You could use tools like *'Calendly'* so that clients can easily book meetings with you, and it stops many of the back-and-forth emails to arrange a convenient time and gets you closer to sealing the deal quicker.

4. Check the spelling/grammar in your proposal, so it is professional.

5. In your proposal, mention other solutions you offer *(upsell as a bundle, or this provides knowledge for the future should the client wish to use these services).*

6. In the proposal, show the gains and benefits for the client constantly, and make the proposal tailored and relevant to them *(it's not about you or your business, but about how you can meet their needs).*

7. Don't use jargon or technical terms in your proposal. It is crucial to

align the communication/jargon based on the target audience who will read the proposal.

8. When pitching a proposal, deliver an experience using stories, analogies, metaphors, and props. If there's anything the client can take away, this is good. Keep your pitch simple. When using Power-Point, use images and a few words on the slides. Ensure your pitch focuses on how you will solve the client's problems and address their needs.

7

HOW TO CREATE CREDIBILITY
AND MARKET YOUR VALUE

This final seventh step is about creating credibility and marketing your value. In this chapter, we will take a look at the '4 Ps' of marketing, and I will show you how you can apply them to your new business. We will learn about branding, creating an online presence, positioning, and marketing the value of your consulting service.

You can trust me on this one; building your own consulting firm from scratch goes far beyond leveraging your expertise to help companies to perform better. You will be forced out of your comfort zone daily. You will need to take paths that you have never taken before. But trust me when I say that this has been the most rewarding life experience; it has made me not only a better professional, but also a better human. If you follow these steps and do the work, I can assure you that your business will be set up for the long run. Let's dive into this last step!

By the end of this chapter, your will know how to:

1. Use the 4Ps of marketing to your advantage.

2. Consider branding but make this more about you and your service initially.
3. Create an effective online presence.
4. Position and market your value.
5. Market a consulting service.
6. Follow the dos and don'ts pro tips from experts.

UNIQUE SELLING POINT (USP)

When building your consulting firm, you need to understand that you are not just a consultant. You are an entrepreneur in charge of every aspect of your business *(especially at the beginning)*. You need to invest time and energy in selling your services, but before crafting a marketing strategy, you need to take a step back and identify your USP.

Every consulting business needs a USP. It makes you stand out as different, better, and more appealing to the client from all of the other consulting companies in your sector in the marketplace.[1]

Determining your USP and the vision you want for your consulting firm can take some time, but trust me, this will pay off in the long run. It could be your skills, experience or expertise, or an approach that makes you different.

For example, you could offer more flexible working hours than competitions or include a free service with your projects *(ensure you have this in your marketing strategy)*.

MARKETING 4 PS: PRODUCT, PRICE, PLACE, AND PROMOTION

"Put the vast majority of your energy, attention, and dollars into building a great product or service and put a smaller amount into shouting about it, marketing it."

— JEFF BEZOS, AMAZON

You might have heard of the concept of the 4Ps in University, but I think it's worth getting into details as I believe it to be a great strategy to craft your first marketing message.

The 4 Ps stand for:

- Product
- Price
- Place
- Promotion

It's essential that you tackle each concept as an individual piece but also as a whole package where every item interacts with each other. You should also be constantly returning to these over time, adjusting and refining them as your business grows and develops.

Focusing on the 4Ps can help you to pinpoint:

- What clients want and expect from you
- How you can meet their needs
- How the world perceives your product
- How you compare to competitors and stand out from them
- How you communicate with customers

Marketers suggest that there are even more than 4 Ps, with *'people,' 'process,'* and *'physical evidence'* being necessary for marketing too[2]:

1. **People** – who is running the business and having the right people to do so.
2. **Process** – how you'll deliver the service to customers and other methods to ensure the company runs smoothly and effectively.
3. **Physical evidence** – is proof that you provided the service, ideally actual receipts or a contact record, and intangible, which is how the market will perceive your business.[3]

In this chapter, I will mainly focus on place and promotion since I have already covered the other points in the previous chapters.

1. Product

Product refers to the service that you'll provide as a consultant. As discussed earlier in the book in Chapter 2, you need to be filling a need for your clients.

2. Price

You need to think about the actual value of the service *(how much does it cost in terms of human resources and physical resources to deliver your service?)* Also, contemplate the *'perceived value'* – what are customers willing to pay for the service, depending on how this relates to competitors, what you offer that is unique, based on your experience and expertise, and what the financial benefit is to them, based on their expenditure. You can check Chapter 6 for more details on this.

3. Place

The place is where you will market your consulting business. With *'Place'*, you are trying to get the consulting business services you offer in front of the clients who are most likely to buy them. You will need to consider online advertisements, webpages, emails, flyers, word-of-mouth via attending business hub meetings/conferences/talks, and recommendations from previous clients, newspapers, TV ads, etc. You can consider whether people will see your services through a webpage, a smartphone app, or other channels.[4]

4. Promotion

Promotion is how you advertise your consulting business. It could include advertising, PR, and a strategy to show clients why they need your service and why they should pay your prices. It could be an

Instagram campaign, LinkedIn posts, a PR campaign to showcase a service you offer, or an email campaign.

🍃 🍃 🍃

Action Point:

- Have a go at completing the boxes below. Define the 4Ps that you want to keep in mind when marketing your firm

1. Product: what service will you provide to clients?
Example: Providing consultation to businesses as to the local government grants/schemes available to increase their staff training in their sector to help ease skills gaps and shortages.

```
┌─────────────────────────────────────────────────────┐
│                                                       │
│                                                       │
│                                                       │
│                                                       │
│                                                       │
└─────────────────────────────────────────────────────┘
```

2. Price: what will you charge for your services?
Example: $500 consultation - but this will gain the customer a lot of money in grants/schemes. Their workforce will improve their skills as a result, and this will benefit the profitability of the business. It will make the business resilient, sustainable, grow and thrive and make them more competitive internationally.

```
┌─────────────────────────────────────────────────────┐
│                                                       │
│                                                       │
│                                                       │
│                                                       │
│                                                       │
└─────────────────────────────────────────────────────┘
```

3. Place: where will your market your consulting business?

Example: Via business hub meetings; via the Chamber of Commerce; at Business Incubation Centers; Online via website and social media; sector discussion forums etc.

4. Promotion: how will you promote your services?

Example: Targeted social media advertising; email campaigns; local newspapers.

BRANDING

"Your brand is what other people say about you when you're not in the room."

— JEFF BEZOS, AMAZON

Over the years, there has been much research on the importance of branding for businesses. I'm not knocking branding; it has *some* significance; but it is lower than the quality of your job, going above and beyond for customers, and behaving in an exemplary professional manner.

My advice for a brand-new consulting firm would be to aim for sleek and professional looking, but don't invest too much time and effort in this. For a consulting business, rather than your logo, it is crucial to build up your credibility by providing an outstanding service that gets you good references online, via word-of-mouth, and through LinkedIn recommendations. These references and suggestions speak volumes with prospective customers rather than what color or style your logo is.

Throughout my career, I've seen colleagues spend enormous amounts of money in building a *'good-looking'* brand and then realizing that it is not enough to fuel the success of their company. So, don't get lost in branding and make sure that the quality of your work becomes your brand. However, once you are further on the way, it is worth spending some time analyzing how the customers perceive you and create a brand that speaks to them. Indeed, once you have a *'brand'* for your consulting business, you become more than just a *'freelancer'*; you become an entrepreneur with a mindset. Jump back to Chapter 1 of this book if you need to refresh the key things you need to keep in mind regarding *thinking like an entrepreneur*.

Action Point:

Take a piece of paper, and try writing your answer to the following points:

1. Be clear about your business offer – *what is your USP, who is your audience, and what makes you stand out from competitors?*
2. What brand will you have, and how will it appear online and in person?
3. Ensure that your business is registered and officially established, business account, etc.
4. Think about how you can build up your credibility and trustworthiness with your clients. Do you regularly ask clients to write recommendations or complete reviews? What could you do to provide them outstanding service *(not one that is 'just' good enough)?*
5. Market your brand identity with a website and social media *(see the next step in this chapter about creating an online presence).*

CREATING AN ONLINE PRESENCE

Today the Internet helps businesses to connect with clients more accessible than ever in a more integrated way.[5] Companies need to generate engagement, connect with customers, and stay relevant to them.

Three-quarters of customers use websites and over a third use social media.[6] Statistics have shown that people spend 8 hours a day online.[7] So, with that in mind, it makes sense to make your online presence the best it can be. Being online is a perfect way to communicate with clients and express what your business offers and how you're better than competitors.

Be competitive

Today businesses need to be exceptional just to remain competitive.[8] Being present online and offering a standard service is not enough. Many companies nowadays are adopting an omnichannel strategy, which can include 24/7 customer service *(could be using AI and chatbots)* and personalized communication. An omnichannel approach ensures that your physical location, social media, website, and mobile are all connected, and a customer can move seamlessly between them.

An online presence is everything you deliberately put out there, but it also can include things out of your control, such as social media conversations about your business or reviews.

Exploit the potential

In 2019, 3.8 million Google searches occurred every minute! Some of these will be potential clients searching for a consultant business just like yours. 97% of consumers find local research businesses online.[9]

Using your website and social media are perfect platforms to show your USP and your values and get customers to resonate with your services.[10] It allows you to market your business 24/7 all around the world. It is vital to show your values seamlessly and consistently through every touch point a potential customer has with you so that they can resonate with it and clearly understand what you offer.

Make Data and Devices Work for You

When you market your business online, there will be lots of data in the background that you can analyze to see which marketing strategy is most effective for you to push more of your budget into doing more.

As said, just being online is not enough nowadays. Instead, businesses need to create an emotional relationship with their clients and teach them and impart knowledge about their methods and techniques. Sharing knowledge, videos, tips, or even celebrations will help customers to build a rapport with you.

Customers like transparency, honesty, and openness rather than rigid formality. Don't be afraid to show your human side. Try to direct people back to your website from your social media posts. You can share information from other relevant businesses, and it's then more likely that they may share your content with their followers. You could look for relevant blogs or articles, videos, or infographics to share and just add some commentary to the post. You can make good use of Facebook, Twitter, and LinkedIn.

Most of your posts should be informative and relationship-building rather than selling

Having an online digital presence can make you more credible. 83% of consumers request a product or service based on the online information they have found – so you need to ensure you're on as many online sources as possible to be competitive and stand a good chance of finding out about the services you offer.[11] More than half of consumers won't consider a business if it doesn't have a website. Many people will research you before hiring you for your services. Therefore, if you rank highly in search engine results and read good reviews about you and your business, you are legitimate, dependable, and trustworthy. Your online presence needs to be professional and show your expertise and how you stand out from your competitors.

Here are some tips for creating a successful online presence:

1. Make sure your website is user-friendly – *(clean, modern, intuitive, has accessibility options to enlarge text, read text, change font size/color, translation buttons, etc.)* Ensure the content on it is current, accurate, and relevant. Your website could have a blog that gives original, up-to-date content to attract clients. 75% of consumers say they judge a company's credibility based on its website.[12] If you can afford this, it can be beneficial to hire someone with expertise in website design rather than setting up your own. Ensure the content of your website reflects diversity to appeal to as many people as possible.

2. Invest in SEO *(search engine optimization)* – link building, content creation, and keyword research, all of these will help to drive traffic to your website, and more traffic will equate to more clients. Think about common themes/trends that your content is about. It will help your website rank higher *(and hopefully get on the first page)* of search results on Google. Another thing to consider is voice search optimization for things like Alexa, Siri, and other digital assistants.[13]

3. Write a business blog – this will allow you to use more keywords. If you post helpful content that helps clients, this will also build your credibility and show you are an authority on the topic you consult.

4. Use social media – If people follow you on social media, 91% of people visit your website, 89% buy from the brand, and 85% recommend it to family or friends.[14]

5. Try to ensure that you are using the platforms that your audience looks at – *"If you want to catch fish, fish where the fish are."* It is better to have one or two social media accounts that you fully engage with rather than be spread across too many and not be active on them. You could consider LinkedIn, Facebook, Instagram, Twitter, YouTube, Pinterest, TikTok, and Snapchat. Being busy is essential, so you must post regularly by addressing educational information and pain points that your service offers and respond to and like the comments from other people. If you can only manage to be active on one account, it's better to do this thoroughly and adequately than spread yourself too thin.

6. Just having a lot of followers' isn't a guarantee of success – You need to have followers engaging with you, so ensure that you target the niche audience that is relevant to you and them.

7. Using emotion to make your followers' feel is essential to engage them in social media content – Emotional words, phrases, emojis, and evocative images all help. Statistics prove that posts with emotion are far more shared.

8. Use hashtags on social media – A hashtag *(#)* allows your content to be discovered by an audience looking specifically for that. The hashtag symbol is used, followed by a keyword or phrase *(you can't use symbols or punctuation in a hashtag)*. There's no cost to use them, but it's sensible to research trends, and when someone is interested in your topic, they can find it easily via a hashtag. It will make your post stand out and get interaction from interested people. Be straightforward with them, not too obscure. Don't overuse them. Generally, one to three is sufficient.[15]

9. Get yourself listed in online directories relevant to your consulting business – Google My Business Profile is essential; there is also Yelp *(used by Alexa and Siri)*. On Facebook, put your business page to *'local business'* or *'place'* to add a location and collect reviews. Be present on Bing and Foursquare. Ensure that your listings are thoroughly populated to help with algorithms.[16]

10. Proactively request reviews so that you keep getting these from clients constantly

11. Use paid advertising to show up in search engines and social media, and websites

12. Use email marketing – 99% of email users check their emails every day *(sometimes 20 times a day)*. It is sensible early on to gain a client's name and email, but if possible, try to find out their challenges and the support they need. Please write a good subject line to get people to open the email, build your email list, and segment it so that you target your audience accordingly.[17] Don't make this too lengthy, and ideally, have it visually appealing and very easy to use.[18]

13. Use guest posts on your blog, websites, and social media, because links from their site to yours can help your SEO

14. Videos are super popular – they are 1200% more shared than simply text and an image. People retain 95% of what they watch in a video, whereas only 10% of the text is read. In the US, YouTube is the most popular platform *(followed by Facebook)*. You could create a YouTube channel and put videos on your website or blog posts, or social media posts. You could do live streaming. You could do TikTok videos; or create Facebook, Instagram, or LinkedIn Stories.[19]

15. The more people you can connect with, the better – so asking loyal customers to write reviews and share posts will help. Influencers could help you reach the audiences you want to. Other business owners could share their tips for success.

16. Ensure that your marketing is suitable for mobile phones – 60% of Internet searches are on mobile devices.

17. Have 'social proof' by posting about events you're speaking at, and display trust seals and certifications – The testimonies, feedback, reviews, and success stories will all help.

❧ ❧ ❧

Action Points:

Checklist to asses your online presence

1. Do you have a website?
2. Do you have a blog?
3. Have you invested in SEO?
4. Have you considered voice search optimization?
5. Is your business active on social media?

6. Do you use emotion and hashtags in your posts?
7. Are you listed in online directories?
8. Do you have a process for requesting reviews/feedback?
9. Do you use paid adverts?
10. Do you use email marketing?
11. Do you use guest posts?
12. Have you made videos?
13. Do you network/make connections?
14. Is your marketing suitable for mobiles?
15. Is there social *'proof'* online?

POSITIONING AND MARKETING YOUR VALUE

You need to know the market trends and who your competitors are. By doing this, you can determine your Unique Selling Point *(USP)* and compare it to your competitors.

It's very easy to underestimate and under-communicate the value you offer to clients. Especially when you aren't selling a *'product'* but services that are based on knowledge, intellectual capital, and experience. I recommend thinking about the years you've spent gaining specific qualifications when you're contemplating your value and use this experience when positioning and marketing yourself. A client will hire you because you have these skills and knowledge gained over time, so it's cheaper to hire you for a small amount of time than it is for them to acquire these skills/experience themselves.[20]

Listen to your client and challenge

Clients aren't buying a service from you as a business consultant. They are buying the outcome of the service. You need to listen to your client's issues and what results they want from you after your consulting services. It's been stressed a lot in this book already, but keep asking your clients questions about their challenges, what they want to achieve, what they want to improve, how improving them will help their business, and what obstacles they have to make your offer valuable to them.

A good suggestion is to ask your customers what would be the cost to the business if they don't hire your services and if they do nothing. What would they be losing out on each month? By engaging in these conversations, you want to show them not only how much money you are saving them but also how much extra money they will make.[21] If, let's say, after your consulting services, your client would get an additional $300,000 each month, it would not be unreasonable for you to charge the client $300,000 for the whole project.

Use the ROI strategy

Getting your clients to talk about return on investment *(ROI)* is helpful because this will create confidence that any money they spend on your services will produce a more excellent value than what they have invested. It will convince them to purchase your services repeatedly. You can ask them what ROI looks like for them, what a successful project would mean to the stakeholders, how it would benefit their customers, how it would give their business a competitive advantage etc.

Practical example

Charles Demontigny, the founder of Fluxion *(a Data Science company that uses AI to help eCommerce companies increase their sales)*, suggests that to position his company to stand out from competitors, he dialed in and optimized his offerings in client interactions. He found it essential to ask his clients lots of questions and use video content whenever possible. Charles's approach when reaching out to potential clients was to reach out to prospective clients and request a 5–10-minute call *(not a lengthy 30-minute one that may put them off)*.

He just wanted to talk with people and see if what he had to offer was a good fit for them; he felt that if it were, they would naturally ask to know more about it. He claims he doesn't have to 'sell' his product; he's explained his offer and asked them questions ... and when it seems a perfect fit, it works.

When dealing with existing clients, he mainly uses video for communication to show a more personal approach. You could use video tools like Loom, BombBomb, or Dubb. By doing this, he differentiated himself from other competitors. Most people email and some *(but few)* pick up a phone and call. A video message is much more visual and allows you to build trust with the client.[22]

🚀 🚀 🚀

Action Points:

- Have a go at completing the boxes below

I. What is your Unique Selling Point? (USP)
Example: A business consultant who works with the engineering sector to improve skills/qualifications of workforce.

2. How do you differ to competitors?
Example: A focus on engineering. Trained as an engineer. Years of experience in HR. Years of experience in government grants/schemes for training. Highly customer focused.

3. What qualifications/experience/skills do you have?

Example: Qualified engineer. Qualified CIPD. MBA qualification. Experience as engineer, and HR Manager. Consultant for 2 local governments.

4. What outcomes will clients get from your services?

Example: previous clients have been awarded funding grants to cover training courses. 10 x members of staff upskilled. 15 members of staff newly qualified. 18 new apprenticeship starts.

5. What would option 1, 2 and 3 be with your services?
Example:

1. *Consultation to discuss training needs of workforce, and information given about grants/schemes to improve workforce skills.*

2. *Consultation to discuss training needs of workforce, and information given about grants/schemes to improve workforce skills, plus 2 workshops delivered to HR staff and Supervisors within the business.*

3. *Consultation to discuss training needs of workforce, and information given about grants/schemes to improve workforce skills, plus 2 workshops delivered to HR staff and Supervisors within the business. Plus 3 months of 1-1 leadership coaching with the 2 Heads of department.*

MARKETING CONSULTING SERVICES

Regardless of how good your consulting skills are, you need to be able to market them to get a steady supply of clients.[23]

Do people know about you? How can they contact you? Research shows that almost 30% of business will tend to come from referrals. Just over 25% will come from word of mouth and 17% from networking.[24] It's necessary to provide an outstanding service for every customer so that when they talk to other people, they are happy to recommend you.

Rather than viewing customers as one-off pieces of work, try to build the relationship and develop trust with them so that they will refer to you and speak of you positively. Nurture the relationship so that if anyone else they know needs your services, you are at the forefront of their mind. It's beneficial to attend relevant events, where you can network with the CEOs and directors of the types of businesses you want to offer your consulting companies to.

Get these online reviews!

Statistics have shown that 88% of customers trust online reviews; this enormous amount shows that reviews can build your credibility.[25]

When marketing your consulting business, you're trying to find clients willing to buy your services. I suggest you should spend 50% of your time doing this. It would be best if you built awareness in your company's clients. You need to make them interested in what you offer and ensure that you stand out from the competition. Ideally, you want people to feel emotionally connected to what you offer. It needs to be easy for clients to contact you and get your service.[26]

Market your consulting services to clients in a way that appeals to them. Some clients will want an individual meeting or a presentation. Other people may like a live demonstration. Other people may prefer to watch a video. So, tailor your marketing to meet your client's preferred method.[27]

*   *   *

Action Points:

Consider the following questions

1. Do people know about you?
2. How easy is it for people to contact you?
3. Do you collect referrals/reviews? Is there a process for this?
4. What could you do to provide a higher quality service for clients?
5. Do you network?
6. Do you build relationships with your clients?
7. Do you need to dedicate more time to marketing your consulting business?
8. Are you targeting sizable businesses for their custom?
9. Are you tailoring how you sell to meet your client's preferred method?

I. Two essential tips from **Larry Page and Sergey Brin**, the co-founders of Google, are *"Always deliver more than expected,"* because by doing this, you can wow your clients. They'll give you great recommendations and referrals, and people will feel they have received great value for money, and this will demonstrate your credibility as a businessperson – someone who goes above and beyond with their service delivery. Their second advice is: *"Invention and marketing are the keys to success."*

2. **Jack Ma**, the founder of Alibaba, when discussing credibility, says about Alibaba, *"We earned the trust of people today"*[28], and gaining people's trust is so essential to achieving credibility and showing your value. In Ma's speech about the IPO, he repeated the word confidence eight times when talking about credibility. Your clients need to trust you implicitly; some of this will come from previous referrals and reviews. Some will come from your online presence and validation. Some will come from word-of-mouth. Some will come from recommendations. A lot will depend on your actions, customer interaction, and high-quality service. By doing this with every customer, you are building up future trust and relationships.

3. One of **Richard Branson**'s key bits of advice is that as a small business, you can take on more prominent businesses, *"We've had a lot of fun taking on fat cat complacent business. What we've done is be the small guy yap-yapping at the big guys taking a small percentage of their market."*[29] Never think that you're not able to approach bigger businesses to gain their customer, even as a start-up, and never be put off by larger competitors. As a smaller business, you may make them your number one priority customer, and making them feel unique and vital can gain their business. Again, Branson talks about Virgin being tiny, and they were *"able to attract the Rolling Stones because they knew they wouldn't be lost on a long list of bigger bands."*[30]

The next chapter will focus on how to grow your business to the next level after following the above seven steps to creating your consulting firm from zero. It will look at expanding and scaling your business to move it on from the start-up phase. It will cover how to differentiate your business and make it stand out. It will include success stories from Consulting Businesses and will summarize what it takes to make your consulting firm a success.

KEY TAKEAWAYS FROM THIS CHAPTER

I. **Be sure of your USP/Vision/Services you provide/competition,** why you stand out, and the benefits of your service to the client.

2. **Remember the 4 Ps** of Product, Price, Place, and Promotion in marketing.

3. **Be outstanding, get excellent reviews, and become the brand for your business** based on your reputation. Be professional. Over-deliver. Get people to know and trust you.

4. **Work hard on your online presence**; it's crucial and will make you more credible, legitimate, and trusted. Utilize a website, SEO, blog, social media, emails, and videos and have social proof.

5. **Don't underestimate your value**, your qualifications, skills, and experience.

6. **Listen to clients and ask lots of questions** about their needs, issues, what they want, and ROI.

7. **Think about how much money your clients can make** as a result of your consulting experience.

8. **Think about three pricing options**, low, middle, and high.

9. Consider using personal touches, such as individual videos, to communicate with clients.

10. Referrals are super important; always provide the highest quality service possible and nurture relationships.

11. Spend 50% of your time marketing.

12. Target large businesses.

8

HOW TO GROW YOUR BUSINESS TO THE NEXT LEVEL

"There are two ways to extend a business. Take inventory of what you're good at and extend out from your skills. Or determine what your customers need and work backward, even if it requires learning new skills. Kindle is an example of working backward."

— JEFF BEZOS, AMAZON

This chapter isn't one of the seven critical steps in the guide to *Start And Grow Your Own Consulting Business From Zero*, but If you've worked through the seven steps, you should be on your way to establishing a thriving consulting business. You can consider this chapter an additional bonus that will support you in growing your business to the next level.

By the end of this chapter, you will know how to set a path for success, not just to achieve your SMART goals with your consulting firm but also to take your business to the next stage of success.

. . .

In this chapter, you will find lots of information I have already covered in detail, such as marketing, social media, and how to identify your target audience. It would be best if you had had the time to familiarize yourself with these and start structuring your thoughts to put these concepts into practice. The most significant changes do not happen overnight; therefore, you should be kind and allow yourself the time to digest this multitude of information, so take some time to go back to previous chapters and use them as crucial pillars to starting your own consulting business.

If you still have any further questions or queries, you are always welcome to contact me via email at: matthew@theconsulting-club.com

WHAT DOES IT MEAN TO TAKE YOUR BUSINESS TO THE NEXT LEVEL?

"If you start thinking you are good at something, that's often the day you stop trying to be better and open the back door for someone to come after you. That's why we always aim higher. We never feel like we're done."

— DREW HOUSTON, DROPBOX

It is very common to read about business people that take their businesses to the next level, but in practical terms, what do they mean by that?

Taking a business to the next level is about ensuring your business continues to thrive, grows, develops, keeps moving forward, strives for continuous improvement, and focuses on the customer's needs. It would be best if you made yourself indispensable to your customers so that they come to rely upon your expertise and work together long-term.

I am very aligned with the educator, entrepreneur, and researcher Juan Navarro who suggests that:

"taking your business to the next level should be a permanent goal in the mind of an entrepreneur and a powerful reason to invest a smart and dedicated effort to achieving business growth."[1]

He suggests that you should constantly be innovating and trying to achieve goals daily to strive towards your vision of future success. For him, taking a business to the next level means making it sustainable and resilient, plus being able to grow and expand. He suggests that the steps needed to reach sustainable growth include talking to your customers, analyzing your competitors, listening to your team, networking, and thinking outside the box.

It's also crucial to *know* what the next 'level' should look like. Please take a moment to reflect on what you mean by it. You need to be specific *(returning to the idea of the 'smart goals')* with something that can be measured when you reach it; otherwise, it's just a meaningless catchphrase. *"So next time you want to take the magic business elevator to the top, stop and determine what all the floors are between you and the penthouse."[2]* If you want to take your business to the next level, you need to think about which factors and numbers work for you for growing the:

1. Number of customers
2. Amount customers spend on services per month/year
3. Locations/areas that you provide your consulting business in
4. Customer satisfaction
5. Customer retention

It would be best to consider the resources and costs needed to achieve this growth. Once you have concrete goals, put a strategy in place, like the *'work back plan'* also known as the Amazon Strategy.[3] The Working Backward method suggests starting by imagining the end product ready to go on the market and drafting a press release about it. In the press release, the product should have a name, intended customer, a problem the product solves, benefits to the customer, and a quote explaining the reasons for developing the product. The press release allows you to run the idea to see if it's viable and well thought through; if it seems to be, the press release keeps the project on target.

∾ ∾ ∾

Action Points:

- What do you class as the *'next level'* – what does it look like? How will you measure this?
- What will your strategy be to grow your business to the next level? What is your Working Backwards *(Amazon Strategy)* plans to make this happen?

HOW TO EXPAND YOUR SMALL BUSINESS

The advice below includes things that I've learned and have leveraged from other entrepreneurs or tips that I have found helpful from my own experience of expanding and scaling my small consulting business:

Up-to-Date Knowledge

Constantly strive to improve your knowledge about your business, issues in your field, technology that relates to it, and understanding of issues that relate to your clients. It would be best if you tried to learn one new thing daily to keep expanding your knowledge and constantly update yourself. You can take part in a training course, gain a mentor or coach, attend conferences, and read the latest news/papers/reports relevant to your area. By keeping up with cutting-edge developments in your field, you will stay current for your clients and constantly evolve, develop, and become more successful.

Be Obsessed with Delegation

"I want to clear my life to make it so that I have to make as few decisions as possible about anything except how to serve this community."

— *MARK ZUCKERBERG, META*

As your business develops and becomes busier, you can only do so much as one person. You need to master the art of delegation. It will help if you delegate everything outside your core competencies that do not maximize your full potential. You need to build, grow and empower a team *(freelancers, associates, or temporary workers).*[4] Even if it takes time to automate every possible task, slowly work towards achieving it. Find the right experts you can trust to do work tasks for you, and be clear about your expectations and timelines.

If any jobs fall out of your core competencies; or are pretty repetitive, then these are the jobs you could get assistance with to free up your time for decision making, development, and strategic thinking.

Sometimes it could take you longer to try to do a job yourself because you don't have the skills/experience that another person has – so it can be better to pay someone to do it rather than do it yourself. If you try to do it all, you run the risk of becoming stressed and exhausted.

Insufficient delegation can impact the quality of your work. You are never going to be an expert in every field, so choose your battles wisely.

Draw upon the expertise of a skilled team

Part of drawing upon expertise can come from building and

retaining a skilled team around you to help you achieve your business goals of expanding and scaling up.[5]

To keep top people on your team, you must ensure a great workplace culture, decent pay, and show appreciation for their work. It would help if you showed gratitude to make your team feel valued and motivated. Remember that your employees are your first customers and that finding and hiring the right people has never been more challenging than in our time due to the fierce competition within the market.[6]

Some advice to attract talent includes responding to talented candidates swiftly. You could consider hiring remote employees to broaden the scope of finding the best or offering a flexible working environment that provides some office time and some remote working as this may appeal to candidates.[7]

Let candidates have challenges to work on and show appreciation for their work. Build your brand from the outset of your business to attract better talent, and be clear about your mission and vision statement.

Be Efficient and Productive

Look at the task you do regularly and see if you can streamline these processes to make them run more efficiently. Some of this may be about being super-organized and having things filed meticulously; some could be a workflow and setting a routine to follow each time consistently.

You may need to upgrade or add resources to help your business grow – spending money on IT equipment that will improve your service could be a worthwhile investment.[8] You could use software tools like ASANA and Slack. Many highly skilled consultants like McKinsey, BCG and Deloitte use these. They use them to keep track of what they need to do and by what deadlines. These software platforms allow international teams to work together on projects despite the different time zones, improving team effectiveness and productivity by up to 25%.[9]

Many places use Outlook email, PowerPoint, and Excel spreadsheets for project plans, but knowing which version is the most up-to-date can get confusing. Software like Asana and Slack shows who is doing what and when, it's effective communication and saves time, and it lends structure to tasks.

Make Good Use of IT

It's essential to keep up to date with technological changes and how this can impact your business. Using IT to track finances, budgets, purchase orders, deal with HR functions, or advertising via social media, etc., can make processes smoother or more effective.

When you know what other technology exists, this opens up options for you or your clients, which may be able to save time, money, or resources. You could consider IT wise if you don't already have them: cloud computing to make your business flexible and scalable; automation software; productivity tools; data security software; and CRM software.[10] CRMs by Salesforce and Quickbooks can help with accounting; InfusionSoft can help with sales and marketing, just a few examples.[11]

🖉 🖉 🖉

Action Points:

- Go ahead an fill in the boxes below with your answers

1. What is your goal or goals?
Example: To increase customers I provide consultancy to, up to 12 customers, who are spending ideally $2000 per month.

2. How can you improve your service to clients?

Example: I could provide more funding information. I could provide more visually appealing documents/reports/presentations.

3. How do you keep up to date?

Example: Attend meetings/conferences/read relevant white-papers, study for qualifications in own time.

4. Do you delegate/use experts?

Example: Yes we use experts for web design, and for data analysis.

5. Are there any processes you could improve to be more efficient/productive?

Example: When requesting delegates for workshops/conferences this could run more smoothly – perhaps by using a CRM/workflows.

6. Are you making the best use of IT?

Example: May invest in a CRM – and need further training on desk-top publishing and social media.

7. Try and test new marketing strategies

Example: Would like to try the effect of short videos on perhaps YouTube or TikTok.

HOW TO DIFFERENTIATE AND EXPAND YOUR CONSULTING BUSINESS

"Business is a marathon, and most of society thinks it's a sprint."

— GARY VAYNERCHUK

You can compare this entrepreneurial journey to running a marathon. Marathon runners can't just run the marathon instantly. They need to build up the strength to do it over a long period. After putting in a lot of hard work, training, and dedication, they can finally participate in the marathon, which is a challenge in itself.

Differentiation is about standing out from the competition

You don't only need to stand out, but you need to do it in a meaningful way for your clients. Differentiation is key because, while you may get referrals from friends/word-of-mouth, these people won't provide you with business forever. You need to attract your own clients as well and make them choose you over someone else.

Price, location, relationships, customer service, process, personality, and awards can help differentiate your consultancy business. But the key, most important thing, should be your core product/service! It is your expertise, advice, and service that people will pay for.

Growing isn't always about scaling up

Maybe you are simply becoming more profitable, generating more revenue, gaining more market share, growing your brand as the best in the area, becoming more influential, etc.

However, if your goal is to scale up and create many jobs for others, consulting companies can do this relatively quickly. A key example is Chris Evans, the co-founder of Traffic and Funnels. Within four years, they grew their startup to have 30 employees and an 8-figure annual revenue; they offer training and mentorship.

Some essential tips for doing this are:

1. Charge a premium price for the service you offer – believe in yourself to do this, and the more you charge, the fewer clients you need per year to meet the target you're aiming for.

2. Ensure monthly revenue is consistent – without prominent, drastic peaks and troughs.

3. Keep focused on your main revenue stream until it's stable – avoid getting distracted. Focus on one area and grow that until it generates consistent monthly revenue.

4. Work on building relationships – try to listen to clients rather than talk to them. Active listening to their needs and objectives, and then in a second step, tailor your message to their concerns. Keep up connections, even when you're not doing any work, to be constantly on their radar.[12] Consultancy is about building trust, which is more important than trying to achieve sales. *"A good consultant is a good marketer of their expertise."*[13] Keep language free from jargon and ensure that content gives value to the reader. Creating this level of reputation and trust will take time.

5. Be flexible – and be prepared to use different business models if they suit your business better. Be relaxed about the staff you hire to help you provide a service with the support of contractors and consultants.[14]

6. Keep track of income/expenditure – Be fully aware of what income you have coming on, and if you're spending money, know what it is being spent on. Keep cash in reserves. Ensure you're making a decent profit.

7. Have a mentor – this should be someone who is an expert in an area that you haven't mastered yourself yet.[15] At the same time, this next bit isn't a *'mentor'*. You can keep an eye on competitors, not overly concerned, to see if you can learn from what they're doing to grow their business.[16]

8. Be an Expert – you need to aim to become a *'thought leader.'* It would be best if you gained the recognition to be seen as an expert in your area, which will make your brand better known and will lead to more income. Online content will help more people to *'engage'* with your sites. You can publish content, speak at events, and lead workshops.[17]

9. Don't try to emulate a larger counterpart – if you're a smaller consultancy business, don't pretend to be something you're not. It is not a disadvantage to be small. Being small, you can offer more personal 1:1 time to clients. Regardless of the size of the business, if you have skills and a fantastic reputation, that is all that matters. Show that you have the flexibility that larger organizations don't have. Pia Silva talks about staying small like *'David'* and *'Crushing Goliaths.'*[18]

ᗺ ᗺ ᗺ

Action Point:

Checklist

1. Does your core product differentiate you from competitors?
2. Do you have expertise, advice, a specialism?
3. Are you charging premium price?
4. Is your monthly revenue consistent?
5. Are you working to build relationships?
6. Are you ready to grow your team?
7. Could you use a different business model?
8. Do you keep track of income/expenditure?
9. Do you have a mentor?
10. Do you present your business as an expert?
11. Are you ready to collaborate?
12. Could you expand services?
13. Have you asked connections to recommend you?
14. Are you honest in your business presentation?
15. Do you use attraction marketing?

CONCLUSION

With this book, I aimed to walk you through a journey. You now have the tools and the combined benefit of my experience as an accomplished consultant, plus the deep researched information from international business people – the giants of internationally renowned companies you'll have heard of- to springboard your consultancy business to be an incredible success.

The seven steps have taken you through:

Step 1: thinking like an entrepreneur, being prepared to work incredibly hard and make sacrifices, and learning from any failures by picking yourself up and ensuring you don't repeat the same mistake.

Step 2: Assessing your expertise and niche. You need to have a good area of knowledge and a clear idea of who your clients will be and what issue or problem your consultancy business can solve for them. You need to create a clear value proposition, mission, and SMART goals you can work towards to achieve success.

Step 3: You must ensure you have followed all legal regulations to be fully compliant, registered with appropriate bodies, and pay taxes accordingly.

Step 4: You need to have meticulously worked out costs and how you will finance your business.

Step 5: Clients are the most valuable asset to your business, and you need to constantly strive to build even better relationships to retain your clients, get more out of them, and get good recommendations, which will help you gain new clients.

Step 6: You need to be clear about your proposal to clients and how you will communicate this to them. It would be best if you were clear about your pricing structure.

Step 7: It would be best if you took the time to develop credibility as this is crucial for a consultancy business; your clients need to trust you implicitly. You, as a consultant, are the leading 'brand' of the company. It's essential to build up an online presence around the service you can provide and the extent to which it addresses the issues of your prospective clients so that they know what is in it for them, and this online presence will boost your credibility. You'll need to give thought to how you can constantly keep your business current relevant, always striving to improve it, and offer an even better service than before, retain previous clients, gain new ones, and make your business more profitable.

What is next?

This book has taken you, step-by-step, through the stages of the journey to make this an achievable reality.

It's now up to you to work through the seven steps and transform your life. You can make a move with confidence from a corporate 9-5 job to becoming a business owner and entrepreneur. I am fully aware that it is a lot of hard work, and you'll inevitably need to make some sacrifices along the way, but there is no better feeling in the world than the feeling that comes from running your own business. Every dollar that you make, you have personally earned, and any money you spend is to build a better business and a better future. The enormous amount of satisfaction that you get when you see that you have made an impact on your customer's business and growth. When clients recommend you to others and want to work with you again in the future, it is rewarding, and you feel appreciated and valued. You have all the tools, now go out there and use them!

If you want to learn more, you can see the website of the consulting club here: https://theconsultingclub.com/ or email me at: matthew@theconsultingclub.com.

A Favor to Ask

If you have enjoyed this book, I'd be very grateful if you could take a few moments to leave a review on Amazon. By doing so, it will help Amazon to let other people who are interested in starting a consulting business know about the book. My goal is to make a positive impact in the world. I want to help as many people as possible to become consultants and start their entrepreneurial journey by mastering the art of consulting. When people pass on their expertise to businesses, and the corporations thrive and grow, this also creates a better economy around us, more jobs, and better communities; in short, help to make the world a better place.

NOTES

INTRODUCTION

1. Mentor Works Ltd, 2021.
2. Riserbato, 2021.
3. Mentor Works Ltd, 2021.
4. GrowThink, 2022.
5. GoCardless, 2021.
6. Consultancy.uk, 2020
7. Hoffman, 2018.
8. Duncan, 2021.

1. THINKING LIKE AN ENTREPRENEUR

1. Neck et al., 2019.
2. Agarwal, Anil, 2022.
3. Zulvia et al, 2018, p.678.
4. Bornancin, 2021, p.119.
5. Marble, 2022.
6. Weinberger, 2018.
7. Bornancin, 2021, p.72.
8. Warren, 2015.
9. Sinek, 2020.
10. Warren, 2015.
11. Dunlop, 2021.
12. Weinberger, 2018.
13. Agarwal, Anil, 2022.
14. Korey, 2018.
15. Barman, n.d.
16. Korey, 2018.
17. Mimaroglu, 2016.
18. Lewis, 2020.

2. THE BASICS: ASSESS YOUR EXPERTISE AND DETERMINE YOUR NICHE

1. Tariq, 2020.
2. Wool, 2022.

3. International Directory of Company Histories, 1994.
4. Hopper, 2021.
5. Just Entrepreneurs, n.d.
6. Hopper, 2021.
7. Shewan, 2022.
8. Osterwalder, 2015, p.14.
9. Jasper, 2019.
10. Shewan, 2022.
11. Osterwalder, 2015, p.7.
12. Searcy, 2022.
13. De Haaff, 2017.
14. Forstadius, 2021, p.2.
15. Forstadius, 2021, p.2.
16. Dobrowolski, et al, 2021.
17. Marquit, 2022.
18. CFI, 2022.
19. Agarwal, Anil, 2022.
20. Tariq, 2020.
21. Osterwalder, 2015, p.8.
22. Osterwalder, 2015, p.40.
23. Osterwalder, 2015, p.8.
24. Outcry, 2018.
25. Bain & Company, 2018.
26. Berry, 2022.
27. Cox, 2022.
28. *(Berry, 2022, online)*
29. Laja, 2019.
30. Salesforce, 2022.
31. Laja, 2019.

3. COMPANY CREATION 101: LEGAL STUFF YOU SHOULD CONSIDER

1. Aha, 2022.
2. Aha, 2022.
3. Jantsch, n.d.
4. Jantsch, n.d.
5. Stowers, 2022.
6. StartupDaddy, 2009.
7. Stowers, 2022.
8. Stowers, 2022.
9. Murray, 2020.

4. MONEY TALKS – HOW TO FINANCE YOUR BUSINESS

1. D'Angelo, 2021.
2. Chen, 2022.
3. Kappal, 2021.
4. Freedman, 2022.
5. Morah, 2021.
6. Berry, 2011.
7. Berry, 2011.
8. Morah, 2021.
9. Startup Donut, 2022.
10. Kappal, 2021.
11. ProfitableVenture, 2022.
12. Startup Donut, 2022.
13. Tan, 2019.
14. Davidson, 2019.
15. Davidson, 2019.
16. Bobbink, 2020.
17. Kobleski, 2022.
18. Investopedia, 2021.
19. Kobleski, 2022.
20. Kobleski, 2022.
21. Bobbink, 2020.
22. Kobleski, 2022.
23. Bobbink, 2020.
24. DowJones, 2022.
25. Investopedia, 2021.
26. D'Angelo, 2021.
27. Zipursky, n.d.
28. ICSTD, n.d.
29. ICSTD, n.d.
30. Belvedere, 2019.
31. Loose, 2021.
32. Bosa, n.d.

5. CLIENT'S FIRST

1. Emberton, 2022.
2. Steimle, 2014.
3. Tull, 2021.
4. Emberton, 2022.
5. Steimle, 2014.
6. McCormick, 2022.
7. Emberton, 2022.

8. Tull, 2021.
9. Tull, 2021.
10. Steimle, 2014.
11. Tull, 2021.
12. Emberton, Oliver, 2022.
13. Emberton, 2022.
14. Tull, 2021.
15. Joon, 2022.
16. Plaksij, 2022.
17. Plaksij, 2022, online.
18. Blankenship, 2022.
19. Blankenship, 2022.
20. Baldassarre, 2015.
21. Dhar & Glazer, 2019.
22. McGivern, 1983.
23. Baldassarre, 2015.
24. Keefe, 2019.
25. Delodovici, n.d.
26. Sharma, 2021.
27. Sanow, 2019.
28. Sharma, 2021.
29. Forbes, 2022.
30. Bornancin, 2021.
31. Keefe, 2019.
32. Forbes, 2022.
33. Sanow, 2019.
34. Delodovici, n.d.
35. Baldassarre, 2015.
36. Sanow, 2019.
37. Keefe, 2019.
38. Sanow, 2019.
39. Tull, 2021, online.
40. Kubiak & Weichbroth, n.d.
41. MBO Partners, 2022.
42. Dhar & Glazer, 2019.
43. Ritson, 2021.
44. Sharp, 2020.
45. Platner, 2020.
46. PwC website, 2021.
47. Deloitte, 2014.
48. EY, n.d.
49. KPMG, 2022.

6. IMPLEMENTATION

1. Bit.AI, 2021.
2. Miller, Mary Kate, 2021.
3. Efti, 2022.
4. Miller, Mary Kate, 2021.
5. Efti, 2022.
6. Harnish, 2011.
7. Team Asana, 2021.
8. Sanfilippo, Marisa, 2022.
9. Harnish, 2011.
10. Richard Woodward & Associates, 2022.
11. Richard Woodward & Associates, 2022.
12. Bolger, Tom, and Casey Foss, 2021.
13. Efti, 2022.
14. Efti, 2022.
15. Dixon, Matthew, and Brent Adamson, 2013.
16. Pipedrive, 2022.
17. Strohkorb, Peter, 2017.
18. Keefer, Kaitlin, 2018.
19. Sumrack, 2021.
20. Allen, 2019.
21. Efti, 2022.
22. Efti, 2022.
23. Zipursky, Michael, 2022.
24. Sumrack, 2021.
25. Zipursky, Michael, 2022.
26. Zipursky, Michael, 2022.
27. Zipursky, Michael, 2022.
28. Efti, 2022.
29. Acuity, n.d.
30. Efti, 2022.
31. Efti, 2022.
32. Karpis, 2017.
33. Ghostit, n.d.
34. Hamilton, 2021.

7. HOW TO CREATE CREDIBILITY AND MARKET YOUR VALUE

1. Consulting Success, 2022.
2. Twin, 2022.
3. Smith, 2020.
4. Twin, Alexandra, 2022.
5. Twin, Alexandra, 2022.

6. Paun, Goran, 2020.
7. McCormick, Kristen, 2022.
8. O'Connell, Madison, 2022.
9. McCormick, Kristen, 2022.
10. Paun, Goran, 2020.
11. McCormick, Kristen, 2022.
12. McCormick, Kristen, 2022.
13. Slayton, Emily, 2022.
14. Claravall, Joyce, 2019.
15. O'Brien, Clodagh, 2022.
16. McCormick, Kristen, 2022.
17. McCormick, Kristen, 2022.
18. Slayton, Emily, 2022.
19. McCormick, Kristen, 2022.
20. Sridharan, Mithun, 2020.
21. Sridharan, Mithun, 2020.
22. Demontigny, Charles, 2022.
23. Lyn, 2021.
24. Chiaravalle, Bill, and Barbara Findlay Schenck, 2021.
25. Claravall, Joyce, 2019.
26. Lyn, 2021.
27. Sridharan, Mithun, 2020.
28. Kim, Eugene, 2014.
29. Nicholls, Charles, 2010.
30. Nicholls, Charles, 2010.

8. HOW TO GROW YOUR BUSINESS TO THE NEXT LEVEL

1. Navarro, Juan, 2019.
2. Smithem, Cheryl, 2022.
3. ProductPlan, n.d.
4. Bornancin, Brandon, 2021.
5. Sutevski, Dragan, 2022.
6. McKinsey & Company, 2022.
7. Jadeja, Rakshanda, n.d.
8. MBO Partners, 2022.
9. Paasch, Sebastian, 2018.
10. Sutevski, Dragan, 2022.
11. Adams, R. L., 2021.
12. Steinberg, Scott, 2012.
13. Smeyers, Luk, 2021.
14. Steinberg, Scott, 2012.
15. Basu, Tyler. 2020.
16. Kanya, 2022.

17. MBO Partners, 2020.
18. Silva, Pia, 2018.

BIBLIOGRAPHY

- Acuity Scheduling. (n.d.) Website. https://acuityscheduling.com/
- Adams, R. L. (2021). 15 Strategies for Quickly Expanding Your Business. *Entrepreneur*. Online. 19th March 2021. https://www.entrepreneur.com/article/306049
- Agarwal, Anil. (2022). Top 20 Most Famous Entrepreneurs in the World. What to Learn from Them [2022 Updated List]. 10th May 2022. *BloggersPassion*. Online. https://bloggerspassion.com/famous-entrepreneurs/
- Aha. (2022). What are business models? *Aha*. Online. https://www.aha.io/roadmapping/guide/product-strategy/what-are-some-examples-of-a-business-model
- Allen, Scott. (2019). New Business Owner's Guide to Pricing Strategy. *The Balance Small Business*. Online. 22nd October 2019. https://www.thebalancesmb.com/the-new-business-owner-s-guide-to-pricing-strategy-1201235
- Bain & Company. (2018). *Mission and Vision Statements*. Online. https://www.bain.com/insights/management-tools-mission-and-vision-statements/
- Baldassarre, Rocco. (2015). 10 Ways to Keep Making Your Clients Happier and Happier. *Entrepreneur*. 9th February 2015. Online. https://www.entrepreneur.com/article/242603
- Barman, Himadri. (N.d.) Being an Entrepreneur: Lessons from Failures. Online: https://www.researchgate.net/profile/Himadri-Barman-3/publication/275888301_Being_an_Entrepreneur_Lessons_from_Failures/links/5548b7d60cf2f974b2392fd1/Being-an-Entrepreneur-Lessons-from-Failures.pdf
- Basu, Tyler. 2020. 8 Lessons on Scaling a Consulting Business to $1 Million in Monthly Revenue. *Tyler Basu*. Online. https://tylerbasu.com/scaling-a-consulting-business/
- Belvedere, Matthew J. (2019). Bill Gates: My 'best investment' turned $10 billion Into $200 billion worth of economic benefit. *CNBC*. Online. https://www.cnbc.com/2019/01/23/bill-gates-turns-10-billion-into-200-billion-worth-of-economic-benefit.html
- Berry, Tim. (2022). How to Write a Mission Statement With 10 Inspiring Examples. *B Plans*. https://articles.bplans.com/writing-a-mission-statement/
- Berry, Tim. (2011). How to Estimate Startup Costs. *Entrepreneur*. 20th September 2011. Online. https://www.entrepreneur.com/article/220342
- Bit. AI. (2021). Consulting Proposal: What is it & How to Create it? (Steps Included). *Bit.AI*. Online. https://blog.bit.ai/consulting-proposal/
- Blankenship, Mike. (2022). 9 Sales Prospecting Techniques to Find Your Dream Customers. *Click Funnels*. 10th Jan 2022. Online. https://www.clickfunnels.com/blog/sales-prospecting-techniques/?gc_id=15306730504&gclid=Cj0KCQiAmpyRBhC-ARIsABs2EAr5EmhYmXkYQe0m4yIsqs-OIKZ8OqgMvTX8ka5RoMRqPz9gPZu_Y7PUaAo32EALw_wcB
- Bobbink, Wout. (2020). There are many sources of funding available for entrepreneurs. Which one is the best for your company? *EY*. 15th September 2020. Online. https://www.ey.com/en_nl/finance-navigator/12-sources-of-finance-for-entrepreneurs-make-sure-you-pick-the-right-one

- Bolger, Tom, and Casey Foss. (2021). Demonstrating the financial value of consulting. *WestMonroe*. Online. March 2021. https://www.westmonroe.com/perspectives/point-of-view/consulting-roi
- Bornancin, Brandon. (2021). *Whatever it Takes: Master the Habits to Transform Your Business, Relationships, and Life*.
- Chen, James. (2022). Money Management. *Investopedia*. Online. 25th May 2022. https://www.investopedia.com/terms/m/moneymanagement.asp
- Consultancy.uk. (2020). Five trends shaping the future of the consulting industry. Online. 28th September 2020. https://www.consultancy.uk/news/25670/five-trends-shaping-the-future-of-the-consulting-industry
- Consulting Success. (2022). The Consultant's Marketing Plan and Business Plan. *Consulting Success*. Online. https://www.consultingsuccess.com/consultants-marketing-business-plan#comments
- Consulting Success. (2022). Your USP – Unique Selling Point. *Consulting Success*. Online. https://www.consultingsuccess.com/usp-unique-selling-point
- Corporate Finance Institute (CFI). (2022). Competitive Advantage: The ability of a company to outperform its competitors. Online. *https://corporatefinanceinstitute.com/resources/knowledge/strategy/competitive-advantage/*
- Cox, Lindsay Kolowich. (2022). 27 Mission and Vision Statement Examples That Will Inspire Your Buyers. Online. https://blog.hubspot.com/marketing/inspiring-company-mission-statements
- D'Angelo, Matt. (2021). 10 Tips for Managing Small Business Finances. *Business News Daily*. 21st December 2021. Online. https://www.businessnewsdaily.com/5954-smb-finance-management-tips.html
- Davidson, Ellis. (2019). The Average Time to Reach Profitability in a Start Up Company. *Smallbusiness*. Online. 9th April 2019. https://smallbusiness.chron.com/average-time-reach-profitability-start-up-company-2318.html
- Delodovici, Jason. (N.d). 10 Ways to Keep Clients Happy and Reduce Churn. *All Business*. Online. https://www.allbusiness.com/10-ways-keep-clients-happy-reduce-churn-15361-1.html
- Deloitte. (2014). Clients first – providing what they need. Leading beyond borders. Online. https://www2.deloitte.com/content/dam/Deloitte/global/Documents/About-Deloitte/gx-gr14-leading-beyond-borders.pdf
- Demontigny, Charles. (2022). Positioning Your Consulting Firm for Success. *Consulting Success*. Online. https://www.consultingsuccess.com/positioning-your-consulting-firm-for-success-with-charles-demontigny
- Dhar, Ravi and Rashi Glazer. (2019). *Hedging Customers*. Online. http://spinup-000d1a-wp-offload-media.s3.amazonaws.com/faculty/wp-content/uploads/sites/48/2019/06/HedgingCustomers.pdf
- De Haaff, Brian. (2017). The Obsession Amazon CEO Jeff Bezos Avoids (and So Should You) *Inc*. Online. https://www.inc.com/brian-de-haaff/brilliant-ceos-do-not-obsess-over-competitors-n.html
- Dixon, Matthew, and Brent Adamson. (2013). *The Challenger Sale: How to Take Control of the Customer Conversation*. Portfolio Penguin. Mi Libro
- Dobrowolski, Zbysław, Grzegorz Drozdowski, and Józef Ledzianowski. (2021). "The Competency Niche: An Exploratory Study" *Risks* 9, no. 11: 187. https://doi.org/10.3390/risks9110187
- DowJones. (2022). Amazon.com CEO Jeff Bezos Puts More Money into Business Insider. *DowJones*. Online. https://www.dowjones.com/scoops/amazon-com-ceo-jeff-bezos-puts-money-business-insider/

- Duncan, Sebastian. (2021). Small Business Consulting & When to Use it. *Real Business*. Online. https://realbusiness.co.uk/small-business-consulting-use#:~:text=A%20small%20business%20consultant%20can%20assist%20you%20in%20defining%20roles,in%20the%20best%20way%20possible.
- Dunlop, Josh. (2021). Top 30 Influential Entrepreneurs of All Time. *Incomediary*. Online. https://www.incomediary.com/30-most-influential-entrepreneurs-of-all-time-2/#:~:text=Two%20key%20traits%20of%20all,take%20the%20risks%20they%20do.
- Efti, Steli. (2022). How to sell consulting services. 12 methods you can start using today. *Close*. Online. https://blog.close.com/how-to-sell-consulting-services/
- Emberton, Oliver. (2022). How to win your first clients. *Silktide*. Online. https://silktide.com/blog/how-to-win-your-first-clients/
- EY. (n.d.) EY Private Client Experience. *EY*. Online. https://www.ey.com/en_uk/private-business/client-experience
- Forbes. (2022). 15 Expert – Recommended Strategies for Keeping up With an Ever-Changing Market. Online. 29th April 2022. https://www.forbes.com/sites/forbesbusinesscouncil/2022/04/29/15-expert-recommended-strategies-for-keeping-up-with-an-ever-changing-market/?sh=79558e65547b
- Forbes. (2020). 5 Ways to Engage Consumers on Social Media. Online. 4th December 2020. https://www.forbes.com/sites/square/2020/12/04/5-ways-to-engage-consumers-on-social-media/?sh=25c066c1b3f4
- Forstadius, Henriikka. (2021). *Business Model Design for an International Solopreneur Consultancy*. Haaga-Helia University of Applied Sciences. https://www.theseus.fi/bitstream/handle/10024/513572/Forstadius%20Henriikka.pdf?sequence=2&isAllowed=y
- Freedman, Rebecca. (2022). Best Accounting Software for Small Business. *Investopedia*. 25th May 2022. Online. https://www.investopedia.com/best-accounting-software-for-small-business-5069679
- Ghostit. (N.d). How to Pitch Like Steve Jobs. Online. https://www.ghostit.co/blog/how-to-pitch-like-steve-jobs
- GoCardless. 2021. The multi-billion-dollar world of small business consulting. *Go Cardless*. Online. https://gocardless.com/en-us/guides/posts/the-multi-billion-dollar-world-of-small-business-consulting/
- GrowThink. (2022). How to Start a Consulting Business. https://www.growthink.com/businessplan/help-center/how-to-start-a-consulting-business
- Hamilton, Ian. (2021). Mark Zuckerberg Explains Facebook's Low-Cost Hardware Strategy. *Upload*. Online. 8th March 2021. https://uploadvr.com/competition-facebook-apple/
- Harnish, Tom. (2011). 7 Tips for Proposals, Pitches and Presentations. *Americanexpress.com*. Online. 2nd June 2011. https://www.americanexpress.com/en-us/business/trends-and-insights/articles/7-tips-for-proposals-pitches-and-presentations/
- Hoffman, Erin. (2018). Five Common Misconceptions About Hiring a Management Consultant. *Forbes*. Online. https://www.forbes.com/sites/forbescoachescouncil/2018/11/29/five-common-misconceptions-about-hiring-a-management-consultant/?sh=64a6c456ea1a
- Hopper, Teah. (2021). How to Define Your Target Audience. Teah Hopper. Online. https://www.teahhopper.com/blog/2018/8/8/how-to-define-your-target-audience
- International Directory of Company Histories. (1994). 'McKinsey & Company, Inc. History.' Vol. 9. St. James Press. Online. http://www.fundinguniverse.com/company-histories/mckinsey-company-inc-history/

- Investopedia. (2021). Jack Ma's Worth and Influence. 19th August 2021. Online. https://www.investopedia.com/insights/jack-mas-worth-influence/
- Jadeja, Rakshanda. (n.d) 9 Ways to recruit top talent for your startup. *iSmartRecruit*. Online. https://www.ismartrecruit.com/blog-ways-to-recruit-top-talent-for-your-startup
- Jantsch, John. (N.d). How to Choose the Right Business Model for Your Start-Up. *DuctTape Marketing*. Online. https://ducttapemarketing.com/business-model-start-up/
- Jasper. (2019). The Airbnb Founder Story: From Selling Cereals to a \$25b Company. *Get Paid for Your Pad*. Online. https://getpaidforyourpad.com/blog/the-airbnb-founder-story/
- Jobs, Steve. (2003). Cited in *Business News Daily*. Online. https://www.businessnewsdaily.com/4195-business-profile-steve-jobs.html
- Joon. (2022). The Top 20 Coworking Spaces Across the U.S. Online. https://joon.us/the-top-20-coworking-spaces-across-the-u-s/
- Kanya. (2022). 7 Essential Tips on How to Grow Your Consulting Business. *Business Tech*. Online. 26th February 2022. https://www.hashmicro.com/blog/consulting-business-growth-tips/
- Kappal, Mike. (2021). The Aspiring Entrepreneur's #1 Question: "How Much is This Going to Cost Me?" *Business 2 Community*. 14th December 2021. Online. https://www.business2community.com/startups/the-aspiring-entrepreneurs-1-question-how-much-is-this-going-to-cost-me-02446932
- Karpis, Paulina. (2017). 3 Strategies for Writing Business Proposals from an Amazon Exec. *Forbes*. Online. July 31st 2017. https://www.forbes.com/sites/paulinaguditch/2017/07/31/amazons-director-of-new-ventures-explains-how-to-write-a-business-proposal/
- Keefe, Rose. (2019). 10 Simple Ways Your Agency Can Make Clients Happier. *TogglPlan*. Online. June 3rd 2019. https://toggl.com/blog/how-to-make-clients-happier
- Keefer, Kaitlin. (2018). How to Determine Consulting Fees. *Squareup*. Online. 13th December 2018. https://squareup.com/gb/en/townsquare/consulting-fees?country_redirection=true
- Kim, Eugene. (2014). Alibaba CEO Jack Ma: 'We Earned the Trust of People Today'. *Insider*. 20th September 2014. Online. https://www.businessinsider.com/alibaba-jack-ma-says-he-earned-the-trust-2014-9?r=US&IR=T
- KPMG. (2022). Helping our clients thrive. *KPMG*. Online. https://home.kpmg/xx/en/home/about/corporate-reporting/helping-our-clients-thrive.html
- Kobleski, Karen. (2022). Show Me the Money: 7 Ways to Get Funding for Your Business Idea. *The Muse*. Online. https://www.themuse.com/advice/show-me-the-money-7-ways-to-get-funding-for-your-business-idea
- Korey, Steph. (2018). Why Embracing Failure is Good for Business. *Entrepreneur*. 20th June 2018. Online. https://www.entrepreneur.com/article/315384
- Kubiak, Bernard F., and Pawel Weichbroth. (N.d.) Cross and Up-selling Techniques In E-Commerce Activities. *Journal of Internet Banking and Commerce*. Online. https://www.icommercecentral.com/open-access/cross-and-upselling-techniques-in-ecommerce-activities-1-7.php?aid=38427&view=mobile
- Laja, Peep. (2019). How to Create a Unique Value Proposition (with Examples). *CXL*. Online. https://cxl.com/blog/value-proposition-examples-how-to-create/
- Lewis, Phil. (2020). Why Embracing Failure is a Big Challenge – And How to do it Well. *Forbes*. 30th January 2020. Online. https://www.forbes.com/sites/phillewis1/2020/01/30/why-embracing-failure-is-a-big-challengeand-how-to-do-it-well/?sh=5406d03143e8

- Loose, Terence. (2021). 10 Genius Money Tips from Billionaire Bill Gates. *GoBankingRates*. 22nd July 2021. Online. https://www.gobankingrates.com/net-worth/business-people/things-bill-gates-says-to-do-with-money/
- Lyn. (2021). How to Market Your Consulting Business Effectively. *ConsultPort*. Online. 6th July 2021. https://consultport.com/for-consultants/how-to-market-your-consulting-business-effectively/
- Marble, Darren. (2022). Jeff Bezos Quit His Job at 30 to Launch Amazon – Here are the 3 Simple Strategies he used to Do It. *Inc*. Online. https://www.inc.com/darren-marble/jeff-bezos-quit-his-job-at-30-to-launch-amazon-heres-how-to-know-if-its-right-time-for-your-big-move.html
- Marquit, Miranda. (2022). 5 Factors to Use When Evaluating a Business Opportunity. *Due*. Online. https://due.com/blog/evaluating-business-opportunity/
- MBO Partners. (2022). How to Get my Consulting Business Past the Start Up Phase. Online. 24th February 2022. https://www.mbopartners.com/blog/how-grow-small-business/how-to-take-your-small-business-to-the-next-level/
- MBO Partners. (2020). 5 Easy Ways to Scale and Grow Your Consulting Business. *MBO Partners*. Online. 19th February, 2020. https://www.mbopartners.com/blog/how-grow-small-business/how-to-grow-your-independent-business/
- MBO Partners. (2022). 5 Upselling Tips for Consultants to Generate More Revenue. Online. *MBO Partners*. 10th February 2022. https://www.mbopartners.com/blog/how-grow-small-business/up-selling-tips-for-independent-consultants/
- McCormick, Kristen. (2022). The 25 Best Ways to Increase Your Online Presence (+Free Tools!) *WordStream*. Online. https://www.wordstream.com/blog/ws/2021/05/17/increase-online-presence
- McKinsey & Company. (2022). Leading Off: Essentials for Leaders and Those They Lead. Online. *McKinsey & Company*. https://www.mckinsey.com/~/media/mckinsey/email/leadingoff/2022/01/10/2022-01-10b.html
- Mentor Works Ltd. (2021). Benefits of Hiring a Business Consultant. *MentorWorks*. Online. 24th June 2021. https://www.mentorworks.ca/blog/business-strategy/hiring-business-consultants/
- Metaoups. (2021). Impact of Salesforce Solutions on Businesses. *Metaoups*. Online. 18th April 2021. https://metaoups.com/impact-of-salesforce-solutions-on-businesses/#:~:text=Salesforce%20has%20enabled%20businesses%20to,platform%20and%20showing%20tremendous%20growth.
- Miller, Mary Kate. (2021). Write the Perfect Consulting Proposal: Tools, Examples, and a Template. *Foundr*. Online. 28th June 2021. https://foundr.com/articles/building-a-business/consulting-proposal
- Mimaroglu, Alp. (2016). How Jack Ma Overcame His 7 Biggest Failures. *Entrepreneur*. 9th September 2016. Online. https://www.entrepreneur.com/article/275969
- Morah, Chizoba. (2021). Business Startup Costs: It's in the Details. *Investopedia*. 13thMay 2021. Online. https://www.investopedia.com/articles/pf/09/business-startup-costs.asp
- Murray, Jean. (2020). Changing Your Business Legal Type. *The Balance Small Business*. Online. https://www.thebalancesmb.com/want-to-change-your-business-legal-type-here-s-how-398665
- Navarro, Juan. (2019). 5 Things to Consider to Take Your Business to the Next Level. *Futurpreneur*. Online. 1st October 2019. https://www.futurpreneur.ca/en/2019/5-things-to-consider-for-taking-your-business-to-the-next-level/
- Neck, Heidi M, Christopher P. Neck, and Emma L. Murray. (2019). *Entrepreneurship: The Practice and Mindset*. SAGE Publications.
- Nicholls, Charles. (2010). Six marketing lessons from Sir Richard Branson. *Retail Customer Experi-*

ence. Online. https://www.retailcustomerexperience.com/articles/six-marketing-lessons-from-sir-richard-branson/

- Osterwalder, Alex, et al. (2015). *Value Proposition Design: How to Create Products and Services Customers Want*. John Wiley and Sons.

- Outcry. (2018). 4 Unique Value Proposition Examples to Inspire You. *Outcry*. Online. https://outcry.io/2018/11/08/value-proposition/#:~:text=Slack,and%20where%20you%20need%20it.%E2%80%9D%20-%20https://www.wordstream.com/blog/ws/2016/04/27/value-proposition-examples

- Paasch, Sebastian. (2018). How to use Asana and Slack as a consultant/ professional service employee. *Asana*. Online. 1st April 2018._https://forum.asana.com/t/how-to-use-asana-and-slack-as-a-consultant-professional-service-employee/18963

- Paun, Goran. (2020). Building A Brand: Why a Strong Digital Presence Matters. *Forbes*. 2nd July 2020. Online. https://www.forbes.com/sites/forbesagencycouncil/2020/07/02/building-a-brand-why-a-strong-digital-presence-matters/?sh=6582c3b049f2

- Pipedrive. (2022) The Challenger Sale model: How to lead the conversation. *Pipedrive*. Online. https://www.pipedrive.com/en/blog/challenger-sales-model

- Plaksij, Zarema. (2022). Prospecting: 10 Proven Strategies for Sales Professionals. *SuperOffice*. Online. 28th January 2022. https://www.superoffice.com/blog/prospecting/

- Platner, Ofir. (2020). "Customers first, employees second," is Jack Ma Serious? *LinkedIn*. Online. January 12, 2020. https://www.linkedin.com/pulse/customers-first-employees-second-jack-ma-serious-ofir-platner/

- Product Plan. (n.d.). Working Backwards (the Amazon Method). *Product Plan*. Online. https://www.productplan.com/glossary/working-backward-amazon-method/

- ProfitableVenture. (2022). How Much Does it Cost to Start a Consulting Business in 2022. *ProfitableVenture*. Online. https://www.profitableventure.com/cost-start-a-consulting-business/

- PwC. (2021). Global Annual Review. Online. https://www.pwc.com/gx/en/about/global-annual-review-2021/clients.html

- PwC. (2018). Who do consumers really trust? *Advisory Outlook*. Online. https://www.pwc.com/ng/en/assets/pdf/who-do-consumers-trust.pdf

- Richard Woodward & Associates. (2022). How to pitch and present a winning proposal. Online. https://richardwoodward.com.au/pitch-a-winning-proposal-in-your-next-presentation/

- Riserbato, Rebecca. (2021). The Rewarding World of Small Business Consulting. *Hubspot*. Online. https://blog.hubspot.com/sales/small-business-consulting

- Ritson. (2021). Jeff Bezos's success at Amazon is down to one thing: focusing on the customer. *Marketing Week*. 3rd February 2021. Online. https://www.marketingweek.com/mark-ritson-jeff-bezos-success-focusing-on-customer/

- Salesforce. (2022). Identify Your Customer. *Trailhead*. Online. https://trailhead.salesforce.com/en/content/learn/modules/isv_business_plan/isv_business_plan_target_customer

- Sanfilippo, Marisa. (2022). Tips for Perfecting Your Elevator Pitch. *Business News Daily*. Online. 29th January 2022. https://www.businessnewsdaily.com/4034-elevator-pitch-tips.html

- Sanow, Arnold. (2019). 25 Ways to Keep Customer for Life. *Amanet*. 3rd April 2019. Online. https://www.amanet.org/articles/25-ways-to-keep-customers-for-life/

- Sant, Tom. (2018). *Persuasive Business Proposals: Writing to Win More Customers, Clients, and*

Contracts. 2018. Amacom.

- Searcy, Tom. (2012). Competitive Advantage: How to Define Your Edge. *Inc*. Online. https://www.inc.com/tom-searcy/redefining-your-competitive-advantage.html

- Sharma, Rishi. (2021). Why the Follow-Up is Everything in Business. *Forbes*. Online. 17th February 2021. https://www.forbes.com/sites/theyec/2021/02/17/why-the-follow-up-is-everything-in-business/?sh=5348fba33c8c

- Sharp, Tina. (2020). "Forget about your competitors, just focus on your customers" – Jack Ma, (Founder, Alibaba Group) *LinkedIn*. Online. 28th November 2020. https://www.linkedin.com/pulse/forget-your-competitors-just-focus-customers-jack-ma-founder-sharp/?trk=read_related_article-card_title

- Shewan, Dan. (2022). Pain Points: A Guide to Finding & Solving Your Customer's Problems. *WordStream*. Online. https://www.wordstream.com/blog/ws/2018/02/28/pain-points

- Silva, Pia. (2021). 3 Expert Tips for Thinking Differently as an Entrepreneur (And Why Your Brain's Needed). *Forbes*. 12th April 2021. Online. https://www.forbes.com/sites/piasilva/2021/04/12/3-expert-tips-for-thinking-differently-as-an-entrepreneur-and-why-your-brains-needed/?sh=4d99c8245eff

- Silva, Pia. (2018). How to Stand Out as a Small Consultancy and Crush Goliaths. *Forbes*. Online. 23rd May 2018. https://www.forbes.com/sites/piasilva/2018/05/23/how-to-stand-out-as-a-small-consultancy-and-crush-goliaths/?sh=5b7b55ca1d04

- Sinek, Simon. (2020). Everyone has a WHY. Do you know yours? *Simon Sinek*. Online. https://simonsinek.com/find-your-why/

- Slayton, Emily. (2022). Marketing Tactics for Independent Consultants: Increase Your Online Presence. *Business Talent Group*. Online. https://resources.businesstalentgroup.com/btg-blog/increase-online-presence

- Smeyers, Luk. (2021). How to Stand Out in a Competitive Consulting Market. *Co Match*. Online. May 31st 2021. https://www.comatch.com/blog/why-consultants-need-to-stand-out-in-a-competitive-consulting-market/

- Smith, Allison. (2020). The Marketing Mix: Boos Your Business with the 4Ps & 7Ps of Marketing. *Meltwater*. Online. https://www.meltwater.com/en/blog/the-marketing-mix-4ps--7ps-of-marketing

- Smithem, Cheryl. (2022). What does it mean to take your business to the next level? *Charleston Public Relations & Design*. Online. https://charlestonpr.com/what-does-it-mean-to-take-your-business-to-the-next-level/#:~:text=It%20implies%20that%20you%20have,between%20you%20and%20the%20penthouse

- Sridharan, Mithun. (2020). Value: How to Communicate Your Worth as a Consultant? *Think Insights*. May 26th 2020. Online. https://thinkinsights.net/consulting/communicate-value-consultant/

- StartupDaddy. (2009). How to Write a Business Plan. How to Start a Business. Online. https://www.youtube.com/watch?v=x0y3VgjhGw0

- Startup Donut. (2022). Essential Guide to Financing Your Start-up Business. *Startup Donut*. Online. https://www.startupdonut.co.uk/financing-a-business/essential-guide-to-financing-your-start-up-business

- Steimle, Josh. (2014). 10 Tricks and Tips for Landing Your First Client. *Entrepreneur*. 10th February 2014. Online. https://www.entrepreneur.com/article/231375

- Steinberg, Scott. (2012). 5 Tips for Building a Killer Consulting Business. Inc. Online. https://www.inc.com/scott-steinberg/how-to-build-a-consulting-business.html
- Stowers, Joshua. (2022). How to Start a Business: A Step-by-Step Guide. *Business News Daily*. 14th April, 2022. Online. https://www.businessnewsdaily.com/4686-how-to-start-a-business.html
- Strohkorb, Peter. (2017). The Top 6 Sales Prospecting Methods, including Cold Calling. *LinkedIn*. 20th June 2017. Online. https://www.linkedin.com/pulse/waiting-contacted-buyer-great-sales-strategy-neither-peter/
- Sumrack, Jesse. (2021). Consulting Fees: How Much Should You Charge as a Consultant? *Foundr*. Online. 1st July 2021. https://foundr.com/articles/building-a-business/how-much-to-charge-for-consulting?clientID=82781806.1647013496&userID=uid.82781806.1647013496
- Sutevski, Dragan. (2022). 6 Tips to Take Your Business to the Next Level. *Entrepreneurship in a Box*. Online. https://www.entrepreneurshipinabox.com/24103/6-tips-to-take-your-business-to-the-next-level/
- Tan, Jon. (2019). 69 of the Best Jeff Bezos Quotes (Sorted by Category). *ReferralCandy*. Online. 18th September 2019. https://www.referralcandy.com/blog/jeff-bezos-quotes
- Tan, Wee Liang and Neo, K. B, and Lim, KKT. (2021). Tackling customer pain points one by one: How TranSwap converted banking diehards. Singapore Management University. https://ink.library.smu.edu.sg/cases_coll_all/395/
- Tariq, Aimee. (2020). How to Use Your Expertise to Start a Consulting Business. *Entrepreneur*. Online. https://www.entrepreneur.com/article/345437
- Team Asana. (2022). 15 Creative Elevator Pitch Examples for Every Scenario. *Asana*. Online. 6th May 2021. https://asana.com/resources/elevator-pitch-examples
- Tull, Chenell. (2021). How to Get Clients: 19 Actionable Ways to Get New Clients [Or Your First Client!] 25th September 2021. Online. https://hustletostartup.com/getting-clients/
- Twin, Alexandra. (2022). The 4 Ps. *Investopedia*. Online. 2nd March 2022. https://www.investopedia.com/terms/f/four-ps.asp
- Warren, Renee. (2015). Why Discovering Your 'Why' is the No. 1 Business Move. *Entrepreneur*. March 23rd, 2015. Online. https://www.entrepreneur.com/article/243737
- Weinberger, Mark. (2018). How Entrepreneurs are Leading the Way into the Future. *EY*. 12th June 2018. Online. https://www.ey.com/en_gl/growth/entrepreneurs-leading-future
- Wooll, Maggie. (2022). Wondering what you're good at? Here are 10 ways to figure it out. *Better Up*. Online. 10th February 2022. https://www.betterup.com/blog/how-to-find-what-you-are-good-at
- Zipursky, Michael. (N.D). How to Scale Your Consulting Business to $1M (and Beyond). *Consulting Success*. Online. https://www.consultingsuccess.com/how-to-scale-your-consulting-business
- Zipursky, Michael. (2022) Consulting Fees Guide: How Much to Charge for Consulting (3 Formulas & Examples). *Consulting Success*. Online. https://www.consultingsuccess.com/consulting-fees
- Zulvia, Yolandafitri and Arif, Adrian. (2018). The Role of Core Value, Character andEntrepreneur Leadership towards Successful Entrepreneur. *Advances in Economics, Business and Management, Accounting and Entepreneurship*. Vol. 57. https://www.researchgate.net/profile/Yolandafitri-Zulvia-2/publication/327898877_The_Role_of_Core_Value_Character_and_Entrepreneur_Leadership_towards_Successful_Entrepreneur/links/5bd7e5604585150b2b90c411/The-Role-of-Core-Value-Character-and-Entrepreneur-Leadership-towards-Successful-Entrepreneur.pdf

Made in the USA
Las Vegas, NV
31 October 2023

79898341R00111